DIABETIC AIR FRYER
COOKBOOK FOR BEGINNERS

200 Crispy and Healthy Recipes for the Newly Diagnosed

Manage Type 2 Diabetes and Prediabetes

Nila Mevis

Table of Contents

Introduction

Receiving a diagnosis of diabetes can be shocking at first. With it comes many questions, worries, and unknowns. Many clients come into my office for their first appointment telling me they are afraid to eat anything because they don't want their blood sugar to go too high. They don't know what to eat or when to eat, and are often frustrated and scared this is happening to them.

It doesn't have to be this way. Picking up this book shows that you have the courage to take a step in the right direction to control your diabetes.

We should all take be taking good care of our own general health, through sensible diet and regular exercise, to help prevent the onset of type 2 diabetes, and other related health conditions, as we get older. It's just common sense.

This easy-to-follow, recipe-packed cookbook will help you to guide yourself towards a lifestyle of healthier eating. If you are not diabetic, the recipes are simply a healthy and delicious way to take care of your blood sugar-levels and carb. Intake and prevent obesity. If you are diabetic, these recipes will enable you to live your life to the fullest, and to really enjoy preparing tasty meals that are fun to cook. But before you begin to try out the recipes on your family and friends, you really do need to understand what the condition is all about. We will answer some simple questions for you to help get you started: What are the differences between types 1 and 2 diabetes? Why are lifestyle choices and changes, such as quitting smoking, not drinking too much alcohol too frequently, eating sensibly, and taking regular exercise so important?

Chapter 1: Understanding Type 2 Diabetes

The condition that is commonly known as diabetes occurs when your pancreas does not produce enough insulin — this is a hormone that regulates the movement of sugar into your cells — and your cells react negatively, and respond poorly to insulin, so they take in less sugar.

What is Insulin? How Does It Work?

Insulin is a hormone that comes from the gland that is situated behind and below your stomach (it's called the pancreas). Insulin regulates how your body uses sugar in the following ways:

- Sugar in the bloodstream triggers the pancreas to secrete insulin.
- Insulin circulates in the bloodstream, enabling sugar to enter your cells.
- The amount of sugar in your bloodstream drops.
- In response to this drop, the pancreas releases less insulin.

It's pretty straightforward how it works, but keeping it regulated when you have type 2 diabetes is critical.

Type 2 diabetes is the most common form of diabetes. It is an impairment in the way that your body regulates and uses sugar as a fuel. This condition results in too much sugar circulating around your bloodstream. Eventually, these high blood sugar levels can lead to disorders of the circulatory, nervous and immune systems. In type 2 diabetes, there are, primarily, two problems. These are short-term problems, and long-term problems. That is to say, symptoms, and complications. These are listed to help you to see the differences.

There is no cure for type 2 diabetes. Losing weight, eating well, and exercising can help manage the condition. If diet and exercise aren't effective, you may also need medication or insulin therapy. Please note: No-one should ever undertake any radical diet or lifestyle changes without first consulting a medical doctor. Risk factors for type 2 diabetes include some lifestyle choices that can be reduced or removed entirely when I am talking about "risk factors and lifestyle choices" in this context, I am referring directly to obesity and lack of exercise.

Significant risk factors include:

- Ageing/growing older
- Excess weight, particularly around the waist
- Family history
- Certain ethnicities
- Physical inactivity
- Poor diet

Prevalence: Type 2 diabetes accounts for approximately 90 to 95 percent of all diagnosed cases of diabetes in adults. Research suggests that 1 out of 3 adults has prediabetes. More than one in every 10 adults who are 20 years or older has diabetes. For seniors (65 years and older), that figure rises to more than one in four.

Signs and symptoms of type 2 diabetes develop slowly. In fact, you can be living with type 2 diabetes for years and not even know it! If signs and symptoms are present, they may include some of the following:

- Increased thirst
- Frequent urination
- Increased hunger
- Unintended weight loss
- Fatigue
- Blurred vision
- Slow-healing sores
- Frequent infections
- Numbness or tingling in the hands or feet
- Areas of darkened skin, usually in the armpits and neck

Type 2 diabetes affects your major organs: your heart, blood vessels, nerves, eyes and kidneys. In addition to these effects, factors that increase the risk of diabetes are also risk factors for other very serious, chronic diseases. So, managing diabetes and controlling your blood sugar levels can lower your risk for complications or coexisting conditions as you get older.

Potential complications of diabetes:

- **Heart and blood vessel disease.** Diabetes is associated with an increased risk of heart disease, stroke, high blood pressure and narrowing of the blood vessels and arteries (atherosclerosis).

- **Nerve damage in limbs.** Consistently high blood sugar levels over time can damage or destroy nerves, resulting in tingling, numbness, burning, pain or eventual loss of feeling that usually begins at the tips of the toes or fingers and gradually spreads upward. This puts you at risk of injuring yourself without knowing about it until you are badly hurt.

- **Other nerve damage.** Damage to nerves of the heart can contribute to irregular heart rhythms. Nerve damage in the digestive system can cause problems with nausea, vomiting, diarrhea or constipation. For men, nerve damage may cause erectile dysfunction.

- **Kidney disease.** Diabetes may lead to chronic kidney disease or irreversible end-stage kidney disease, which may require dialysis or a kidney transplant.

- **Eye damage.** Diabetes increases the risk of serious eye diseases, such as cataracts and glaucoma, and may damage the blood vessels of the retina, potentially leading to blindness.

- **Skin conditions** - including bacterial and fungal infections.

- **Slow healing** - untreated cuts and blisters can become serious infections, which may heal poorly. Severe damage to limbs might even require amputation.

- **Hearing impairment** - hearing problems are more common in people with diabetes.

- **Sleep apnoea** - Obstructive Sleep Apnoea is common in people with type 2 diabetes. Obesity may be the main contributing factor to both conditions. This condition is seriously detrimental to overall quality of life, and can cause premature death though heart failure, due to lack of oxygen in the blood.

- **Dementia** - the risk of Alzheimer's disease and other disorders that cause dementia are significantly increased. Poor control of blood sugar levels is linked to a more rapid decline in overall memory, and other critical thinking skills.

What is the Difference between Type 1 Diabetes and Type 2 Diabetes?

The two most common forms of diabetes are type 1 and type 2. Both involve problems with insulin, but the causes of type 1 and type 2 diabetes are different.

People with type 1 diabetes don't produce insulin and they need to rely on insulin injections in order to survive. Type 1 is an autoimmune condition, in which your immune system targets the insulin-producing cells in your pancreas. It has a genetic component. However, not all identical twins get type 1 diabetes, so other factors may play a role in which people are most susceptible to the condition.

People with type 2 diabetes do produce insulin, but they are unable to use their own insulin effectively, either because they don't make enough or because their cells are resistant to the insulin that they do make. People with type 2 can use a combination of diet, exercise, oral medication, and insulin or other injectable drugs to control their blood sugar.

What is a Healthy Diet for Someone with Diabetes?

When you have type 1 diabetes, you can eat pretty much the same diet as anyone else, provided it is a healthy diet that is low in unhealthy fats. There are some rules, that you should follow though:

Meal timing is very important for people. Your meals must match insulin doses. Eating meals with a low glycaemic index makes meal timing easier. Low glycaemic loads raise your blood sugar slowly and steadily, which leaves plenty of time for your body (or the injected insulin dose you take) to respond. Skipping a meal or eating late puts you at risk for low blood sugar (hypoglycaemia).

Foods you should eat if you are type 1 include complex carbohydrates such as these:

- Brown rice
- Whole wheat
- Quinoa
- Oatmeal
- Fruits
- Vegetables
- Beans and Lentils
- Foods that you should avoid if you are type 1 include the following:
- Sodas (both diet and regular)

- Simple carbohydrates - processed/refined sugars, like white bread, pastries, chips, cookies, pasta

- Trans fats (anything with the word hydrogenated on the label) and high-fat animal products. Fats don't have much of a direct effect on blood sugar, but they can be useful in slowing the absorption of carbohydrates.

When you have type 2 diabetes, you should follow a meal plan that includes complex carbohydrates such as those listed above. Foods to avoid include the same simple carbohydrates - such as sugar, pasta, white bread, flour, cookies, and pastries, etc. So, it's similar to how you should eat if you have type 1. A high protein diet provides steady energy with little effect on blood sugar, and can help with sugar cravings and feeling full after eating. Protein-packed foods to eat include beans, legumes, eggs, seafood, dairy, peas, tofu, and lean meats and poultry. All these are easy to cook, easy to access foods. And, if you want to give your diet a boost, there are five diabetes "superfoods" that you can eat, which are very beneficial to the cardio-vascular system, digestion, and general health. These include chia seeds, wild salmon, white balsamic vinegar, cinnamon, and lentils.

As with any healthy-eating program, a healthy diabetes meal plan should include plenty of vegetables, and limit amounts of processed sugars and red meat. For people with type 2 diabetes, dietitians often recommend a vegetarian or vegan diet. If you really want to eat meat, the Paleo Diet, and the Mediterranean Diet are also recommended.

How Much Should I Eat Per Day?

First of all, how many calories you are taking in depends on whether or not you are taking insulin with your meals (type 1.) If you take mealtime insulin, you need to count carbs to match your insulin dose to the amount of carbs in your foods and drinks. You may also take additional insulin if your blood sugar is higher than your target when eating. So, this will affect amounts of insulin that you self-administer on a daily basis.

If you are Type 2, then you are not taking insulin with your meals, so life is a little less complicated. But you still have to count the carbs if you want to maintain your blood sugar levels. Everyone, whether they have type 1 or type 2 diabetes or not, should be eating a balanced, nutritious diet that is appropriate for their age and their activity levels. Staying hydrated is critical too. Drinking lots of water is an important part of maintaining good general health.

Nutrition and Diabetes

Nutrition is not simply about how much you eat, it's also about what you eat. And, as we have touched on already, if you have diabetes, it's also about when you eat. It is probable, if you have type 2 diabetes, that you are overweight. So, losing a few of those excess kilos is absolutely essential. Meal planning is, therefore, very important, because random "grazing" is not a good way to control what we eat. Becoming generally more active, and then making big changes to what you eat and drink can seem very challenging at first. Especially if your bad habits are ingrained. You may find it easier to start by making some small changes, and it won't hurt to get some help and support from your family, friends, and health care team. Eating well and being physically active most days of the week can help you with the essentials of well-being and managing your condition:

- Keeping your blood glucose level, blood pressure, and cholesterol in your target ranges
- Losing weight or maintaining a healthy weight
- Preventing or delaying diabetes problems
- Feeling good and having more energy

You need to eat a variety of healthy foods, from all the food groups, in the exact amounts that your diabetic meal plan outlines.

The food groups are:

Vegetables

- Non-starchy vegetables include broccoli, carrots, greens, peppers, and tomatoes
- Starchy vegetables include potatoes, corn, and green peas

Fruits (oranges, melon, berries, apples, bananas, and grapes etc)

Grains (at least half of your grains for the day should be whole grains)

- wheat, rice, oats, cornmeal, barley, and quinoa
- bread, pasta, cereal, and tortillas

Protein

- Lean meat
- Chicken or turkey without the skin
- Fish
- Eggs
- Nuts and peanuts
- Dried beans and certain peas, such as chickpeas and split peas
- Meat substitutes, such as tofu

Dairy (non-fat or low fat preferably)

- Milk or lactose-free milk if you are lactose intolerant
- Yogurt
- Cheese

Exercise and Diabetes

Exercise is an important part of everyone's healthy life, and it is critical to your diabetes treatment plan. To avoid potential problems, make sure that you check your blood sugar before, during, and after you exercise. This will show you how your body responds to exercise, and this can help you to prevent potentially dangerous blood sugar fluctuations. If you are taking insulin or other medications that can cause low blood sugar (hypoglycaemia), it is vital that you test your blood sugar 15 to 30 minutes before you start exercising. If you don't take medications for your diabetes or you don't use medications commonly linked to low blood sugar levels, you probably won't need to take any special precautions prior to exercising. But it is a good habit to get into anyway. If you are in any doubt, check with your doctor.

Before you get started on your exercise program, ask your doctor how the activities that you're contemplating might affect your blood sugar. The doctor can also suggest the optimum time to exercise, and he can explain the potential impact of medications on your blood sugar as you become more active.

Health experts recommend that everyone, irrespective of whether they are diabetic or not, undertakes at least 150 minutes per week of moderately intense physical activities such as:

- Fast walking
- Lap swimming
- Bicycling

But once you are feeling an improvement in your overall energy levels, and your fitness and stamina has built up, you can take your exercise routine to higher levels. Always remember to check those blood sugar levels and consult your doctor before you make any significant changes.

Tips and Tricks

We have included a couple of easy things that you can do on a day-to-day basis that will make the planning and preparation of your meals so much easier. It's always good to be aware of what you are putting into your body anyway, but it's super-important when you have diabetes. So, understanding what food is made up of is important. You might be surprised by what is in some of those "healthy" foods that you regularly eat!

How to read a label

Understanding the Nutrition Facts labels on pre-prepared and processed food items will help you to make much healthier choices. Labels usually break down the percentages of calories, carbs, fats, fibres, proteins, and vitamins per serving. This makes it easier for you to compare the nutritional content and value of similar products. Look at different brands of the same foods—nutrition information can differ a lot. One brand of tomato sauce may have more calories and sugar than another brand, for the same serving size. Next time you go shopping, look at the labels of the most common items in your cupboards and refrigerator, and compare them with other brands of the same. You can photograph the labels with your smartphone for an accurate comparison with items in the store as you shop.

Counting Carbohydrates

Carb counting simply involves counting the number of grams of carbohydrate that are in a meal and then matching that to your dose of insulin. If you take mealtime insulin, first account for each carbohydrate gram you eat, and dose your mealtime insulin based on that count. It's what's known as an insulin-to-carb ratio, and it calculates how much insulin you should take to manage your blood sugars after eating. This form of carb counting is recommended for people who are on intensive insulin therapy. If you don't need to take insulin, you can do a more basic version of carb counting based on "carbohydrate choices." Put simply, this is where one "choice" contains about 15 grams of carbohydrate. Or, you could try using the Diabetes Plate Method by limiting whole grains, starchy vegetables, fruits or dairy to a quarter of your plate.

Chapter 2: Air Fryer 101

Fried foods are bad for your health

Frying food normally involves some kind of fat; usually vegetable oil. It is heated to a temperature that is around twice that of boiling point. Very hot oil is important, to prevent too much oil being absorbed into the food you are cooking.

Your choice of oil adds a distinctive flavor to your fried food. Commonly used oils are sunflower oil, canola oil, olive oil, peanut oil, and sesame oil.

The oil is just part of the flavor profile of fried foods, though. Most of the irresistible flavor comes from what the heat does to the crumbs or batter that coats the food. The starches in the coating are caramelized, making them slightly sweeter, and more digestible - and don't forget, crunchy.

The combination of the high cooking temperature, the oil itself, and the browning reaction on the surface of the food is what gives fried food its distinctive, irresistible crunch and flavor. But the oil is the reason fried food is bad for our health.

While a moderate amount of fat is important for maintaining health, too much, and the wrong kind of fat, is a problem. Fat is a very dense source of calories, and it can be easy to eat too much, especially if you love fried food. This can make maintaining a healthy weight very difficult.

When oil is heated to the temperatures required for frying food, the chemical structure of the oil becomes denatured. These denatured fats and saturated fats, such as those found in cheese, meat, and chicken skin, contribute to raised cholesterol levels. They raise your risk of developing cardiovascular disease.

That is why your doctor or dietitian will always tell you to cut back on fried food. There is strong scientific evidence to support this piece of advice.

The health benefits of using an air fryer to cook food

Luckily, the clever people who are constantly coming up with new ideas and gadgets for cooking food, invented the air fryer. Now we have a way of cooking our food so that it tastes just like fried food, but with very little fat.

Foods like frozen battered fish, chicken schnitzel, and baked potatoes can be cooked in the air fryer, without adding any additional oil. You may want to mix a little oil with your sweet potato fries, or brush your steak with some oil before cooking it. The amount you need is significantly less than you would use in a deep fryer. All you need is a teaspoon full. This simple fact makes cooking in the air fryer a healthier option.

Tips for air fryer success

Using the air fryer is as easy as 1,2,3. Air fryers come in different shapes and sizes, but they all do the same thing. It is always a good idea to familiarize yourself with your air fryer by reading the user manual. It will save you the frustration of trying to figure it out when you have a hungry family to feed.

You can fry, roast, grill, or bake in your air fryer. It isn't exclusively reserved for making French fries!

Use these tips to make sure you have perfectly cooked, crunchy, scrumptious food every time:

1. Preheat your air fryer if your model requires that it is hot before you put the food into it.
2. Place your food in the air fryer drawer or basket. It should not be more than ⅔ full.
3. Insert the filled drawer or basket.
4. Select your temperature.
5. Set the timer for the desired cooking time. (If your air fryer does not need to be preheated, you can add three minutes to your cooking time instead.)

6.Check the food half way through the cooking time. Remove it from the air fryer, and shake it or move it around, to ensure even cooking.

7.Adjust the temperature, if necessary.

8.Once cooking is complete, remove the drawer or basket from the air fryer, and place it on a heat resistant surface.

There are many ways to make your air fryer the most used appliance in your kitchen.

#1 Invest in some accessories

Accessories are not essential for the everyday use of your air fryer, but they can open up some exciting cooking possibilities. An oven-safe baking dish or cake pan, that fits into your air fryer without touching the sides, means you can cook foods that start off as a liquid. Mini foil pie pans and cupcake liners are also useful.

#2 Adapt your traditional recipes with ease

You are not restricted to cooking food from recipes that have been created specifically for the air fryer. You can easily adapt your old recipes for perfect results in your new favorite appliance. Simply reduce the cooking temperature by 50°F (10°C), and halve your cooking time.

#3 Boost the browning

Most foods need a little help to brown to perfection. That is why some oil is called for in most recipes. Using an oil spray is a handy way of coating the surface of the food with just a little oil. Glazes also add great color to your food, and extra flavor, especially if they contain ingredients like honey, hoisin sauce, or chutney.

#4 Add water to prevent drying

A bit of dehydration on the surface of most of the foods you cook in your air fryer will give you the results you are looking for - brown, crispy food. But some foods, such as vegetables, can dry out a bit too much. To make sure your veggies come out of the air fryer cooked to perfection, add a little water in the bottom of the cooking drawer or basket. That will create a steam-roasting effect, that is a winning strategy for cooking foods that contain a lot of moisture.

#5 Consider using skewers

When your meat, fish, or chicken is cut into smaller chunks, and slipped onto a skewer, more of your meat is exposed to the hot air in the air fryer. Your meat will have more flavor and texture than if you cooked it whole.

#6 Flip your food half way

The heat in an air fryer only comes from the top of the oven. For better cooking results, it is a good idea to flip your food over half way through cooking, so that it browns evenly on all sides.

#7 Single layer of food only

Don't be tempted to cook too much food at once. Best results are achieved if there is only a single layer of food in your cooking drawer or basket. That way, all of the food is evenly heated.

How to clean your air fryer

Unfortunately, the air fryer is not all fun and games. It does need to be cleaned after you use it. Luckily, even though you are making all of your favorite fried foods, there is a lot less oily residue to clean up afterwards. The air fryer is as easy to clean as it is to use.

First, some important notes about cleaning your air fryer:

1.It is an electrical appliance, so whatever you do, don't submerge it in water.
2.Be gentle with it. Avoid using metal utensils, and abrasive sponges or wire brushes to remove cooked food particles. You don't want to damage the non-stick coating in your air fryer.
3.To remove any foul odors, you can simply place half a lemon inside the air fryer for half an hour before you clean it.

The food basket or drawer should be washed with warm soapy water and a soft sponge, after every use. It is also a good idea to wipe the inside of the air fryer with a damp sponge. Make sure to dry the surfaces once they are clean.

<u>Breakfast</u>

Spinach and Mushrooms Omelet

Preparation Time: 15 minutes
Cooking Time: 6 minutes
Servings: 4

Ingredients:

- *½ cup spinach leaves*
- *1 cup mushrooms*
- *3 green onions*
- *1 cup water*
- *½ tsp. turmeric*
- *½ red bell pepper*
- *2 tbsp. butter, low fat*
- *1 cup almond flour*
- *½ tsp. onion powder*
- *½ tsp. garlic powder*
- *½ tsp. fresh ground black pepper*
- *¼ tsp. ground thyme*
- *2 tbsp. extra-virgin olive oil*
- *1 tsp. black salt*
- *Salsa, store-bought*

Directions: Preheat the Air Fryer to 300°F. Rinse spinach leaves over tap water. Set aside. In a mixing bowl, combine green onions, onion powder, garlic powder, red bell pepper, mushrooms, turmeric, thyme, olive oil, salt, and pepper. Mix well.
In another bowl, combine water and flour to form a smooth paste.
In a pan, heat olive oil. Sauté peppers and mushrooms for 3 minutes. Tip in spinach and cook for 3 minutes. Set aside. Put in the air fryer basket our omelet batter. Cook for 3 minutes before flipping. Place vegetables on top. Season with salt. Serve with salsa on the side.

Nutrition: Calories: 108.5, Carbs: 8.4g, Fat: 1.1g, Fiber: 1.0g, Protein: 5.9g

Fennel Frittata

Preparation Time: 5 minutes
Cooking Time: 15 minutes
Servings: 6

Ingredients:

- *1 fennel bulb; shredded*
- *6 eggs; whisked*
- *2 tsp. cilantro; chopped.*
- *1 tsp. sweet paprika*
- *Cooking spray*

- *A pinch of salt and black pepper*

Directions: Take a bowl and mix all the ingredients except the cooking spray and stir well. Grease a baking pan with the cooking spray, pour the frittata mix and spread well.
Put the pan in the Air Fryer and cook at 370°F for 15 minutes. Divide between plates and serve them for breakfast.

Nutrition: Calories: 199.2, Fat: 11.4g, Fiber: 1g, Carbs: 4.7g, Protein: 8.4g

Strawberries Oatmeal

Preparation Time: 5 minutes
Cooking Time: 15 minutes
Servings: 4

Ingredients:

- ½ cup coconut; shredded
- ¼ cup strawberries
- 2 cups coconut milk
- ¼ tsp. vanilla extract
- 2 tsp. stevia
- *Cooking spray*

Directions: Grease the Air Fryer's pan with the cooking spray, add all the ingredients inside, and toss.
Cook at 365°F for 15 minutes, divide into bowls, and serve.

Nutrition: Calories: 141.3, Fat: 6.4g, Fiber: 2g, Carbs: 2.8g, Protein: 5.4g

All Berries Pancakes

Preparation Time: 15 minutes
Cooking Time: 10 minutes
Servings: 4

Ingredients:

- *½ cup frozen blueberries, thawed*
- *½ cup frozen cranberries, thawed*
- *1 cup coconut milk*
- *2 tbsp. coconut oil, for greasing*
- *2 tbsp. stevia*
- *1 cup whole wheat flour, finely milled*
- *1 tbsp. baking powder*
- *1 tsp. vanilla extract*

- *¼ tsp. salt*

Directions: Preheat Air Fryer to 330°F. In a mixing bowl, combine coconut oil, coconut milk, flour, stevia, baking powder, vanilla extract, and salt. Gently fold in berries.
Divide batter into equal portions. Pour into the Air fryer basket. Flip once the edges are set. Do not press down on pancakes. Transfer to a plate. Sprinkle with palm sugar. Serve.

Nutrition: Calories: 57, Carbs: 13.6g, Fat: 0.5g, Protein: 0.9g, Fiber: 2.4g

Scrambled Eggs

Preparation Time: 5 minutes
Cooking Time: 5 minutes
Servings: 2

Ingredients:

- *4 large eggs.*
- *½ cup shredded sharp Cheddar cheese.*
- *2 tbsp. unsalted butter; melted.*

Directions: Crack eggs into a 2-cup round baking dish and whisk. Place dish into the air fryer basket.
Set the temperature to 400 Degrees F and set the timer for 10 minutes.
After 5 minutes, stir the eggs and add the butter and cheese. Let cook for 3 minutes and stir again.
Allow eggs to finish cooking an additional 2 minutes or remove if they are to your desired liking.
Use a fork to fluff. Serve warm.

Nutrition: Calories: 358.3, Protein: 19.8g, Fiber: 0g, Fat: 27.2g, Carbs: 0.9g

Mushroom and Cheese Frittata

Preparation Time: 20 minutes
Cooking Time: 20 minutes
Servings: 4

Ingredients:

- *6 eggs*
- *6 cups button mushrooms, sliced thinly*
- *1 red onion, sliced into thin rounds*
- *6 tbsp. Feta cheese, reduced fat, crumbled*
- *Pinch salt*
- *2 tbsp. olive oil*

Directions: Preheat Air Fryer to 330°F.

Sauté onions and mushrooms. Transfer to a plate with a paper towel. Meanwhile, beat the eggs in a bowl.

Season with salt. Coat a baking dish with cooking spray. Pour egg mixture.

Add in mushrooms and onions. Top with crumbled feta cheese.

Place baking dish in the Air fryer basket. Cook for 20 minutes. Serve.

Nutrition: Calorie: 139.2, Carbs: 5.6g, Fat: 10.4g, Protein: 22.9g, Fiber: 1.2g

Monkey Bread

Preparation Time: 2 minutes
Cooking Time: 7 minutes
Servings: 8

Ingredients:

- *1 cup non-fat Greek yogurt*
- *1 cup self-rising flour*
- *1 tsp. sugar*
- *½ tsp. cinnamon*

Directions: Combine in a medium bowl the self-rising flour and yogurt; mix well to form into dough.

Custom the dough into a large ball and cut into fourths.

Remove each dough wedge to shape into a flattened circular disc, and then cut into eight pieces, similar to a pizza. Remove each wedge from the disc and roll it to form into balls. Combine cinnamon and sugar in a Ziploc or resealable plastic bag. Add the dough balls and seal the bag; shake to coat the balls well. Prepare a mini loaf pan by lightly misting it with non-stick spray.

Arrange the dough balls in the pan and sprinkle lightly with the sugar-cinnamon mix.

Put the loaf pan inside the air fryer. Bake the bread for 7 minutes, at 375°F. Let cool.

Nutrition: Calories: 72.4, Carbs: 14.1g, Fiber: 0.5g, Sugar: 2.2g, Protein: 3.3g

Grilled Cheese Sandwiches

Preparation Time: 2 minutes
Cooking Time: 7 minutes
Servings: 2 sandwiches

Ingredients:

- *4 slices American cheese*
- *4 slices sandwich bread*
- *Pat Butter*

Directions: Warm your air fryer to 360°F. Fill the center of 2 bread slices with two slices of American cheese.

Binge an even layer of butter on each side of the sandwich and position it in the hamper of your air fryer in a single layer. Insert toothpicks on the corners of each sandwich to seal.

Air-fries the sandwiches for 4 minutes, flipping once, and cook for another 3 minutes until toasted.

Nutrition: Calories: 296.8, Fat: 14.4g, Carbs: 30.7g, Fiber: 1g, Sugar: 6.8g, Protein: 12.1g

Asparagus Omelet

Preparation Time: 10 minutes
Cooking Time: 8 minutes
Servings: 2

Ingredients:

- *3 eggs*
- *5 steamed asparagus tips*
- *2 tbsp. of warm milk*
- *1 tbsp. parmesan cheese, grated*
- *Salt and pepper, to taste*
- *Non-stick cooking spray*

Directions: Mix in a large bowl, eggs, cheese, milk, salt, and pepper, then blend them.

Spray a baking pan with non-stick cooking spray.

Transfer the mixture into the pan and add the asparagus, then place the pan inside the baking basket.

Set the air fryer to 320°F for 8 minutes. Serve warm.

Nutrition: Calories: 230.2, Fat: 9g, Carbs: 7.8g, Protein: 12.4g

Pumpkin Pie French Toast

Preparation Time: 10 minutes
Cooking Time: 20 minutes
Servings: 4

Ingredients:

- *2 larges, beaten eggs*
- *4 slices cinnamon swirl bread*
- *¼ cup milk*
- *¼ cup pumpkin puree*
- *¼ tsp. pumpkin spices*
- *¼ cup butter*

Directions: In a large mixing bowl, mix pumpkin puree, milk, eggs, and pie spice. Whisk until the mixture is smooth. In the egg mixture, dip the bread on both sides.
Place the rack inside of the air fryer's cooking basket. Place 2 slices of bread onto the rack. Set the temperature to 340°F for 10 minutes. Serve pumpkin pie toast with butter.

Nutrition: Calories: 211.5, Fat: 7.8g, Carbs: 6.7g, Protein: 11.6g

Cinnamon and Cheese Pancake

Preparation Time: 5–7 minutes
Cooking Time: 16 minutes
Servings: 4

Ingredients:

- *2 eggs*
- *2 cups cream cheese, reduced-fat*
- *½ tsp. cinnamon*
- *1 pack Stevia*

Directions: Preheat Air Fryer to 330°F.
Meanwhile, combine cream cheese, cinnamon, eggs, and stevia in a blender.
Pour ¼ of the mixture in the air fryer basket. Cook for 2 minutes on each side. Repeat the process with the rest of the mix. Serve.

Nutrition: Calories: 139.2, Carbs: 5.2g, Fat: 10.4g, Protein: 22.9g, Fiber: 1.2g

Low-Carb White Egg and Spinach Frittata

Preparation Time: 12-15 minutes
Cooking Time: 12 minutes
Servings: 4

Ingredients:

- *8 egg whites*
- *2 cups fresh spinach*
- *2 tbsp. olive oil*
- *1 green pepper, chopped*
- *1 red pepper, chopped*
- *½ cup feta cheese, reduced fat, crumbled*
- *¼ yellow onion, chopped*
- *1 tsp. salt*
- *1 tsp. pepper*

Directions: Warm the Air Fryer to 330°F.

Meanwhile, place red and green peppers and onions in the Air Fryer basket, and cook for 3 minutes. Season with salt and pepper. Pour egg whites and cook for 4 minutes. Add in the spinach and feta cheese on top.
Cook for 5 minutes. Transfer to a plate, slice, and service.

Nutrition: Calories: 119.5, Carbs: 12.4g, Fat: 4.2g, Protein: 10.2g, Fiber: 1.2g

Scallion Sandwich

Preparation Time: 10 minutes
Cooking Time: 10 minutes
Servings: 1

Ingredients:

- *2 slices wheat bread*
- *2 tsp. butter, low fat*
- *2 scallions, sliced thinly*
- *1 tbsp. parmesan cheese, grated*
- *¾ cup cheddar cheese, reduced-fat, grated*

Directions: Preheat the Air fryer to 356°F.
Spread butter on a slice of bread. Place inside the cooking basket with the butter side facing down.
Place cheese and scallions on top. Spread the rest of the butter on the other slice of bread, put it on top of the sandwich, and sprinkle with parmesan cheese. Cook for 10 minutes.

Nutrition: Calories: 153.5, Carbs: 8.7g, Fat: 2.3g, Protein: 8.9g, Fiber: 2.4g

Breakfast Cheese Bread Cups

Preparation Time: 10 minutes
Cooking Time: 15 minutes
Servings: 2

Ingredients:

- *2 eggs*
- *2 tbsp. cheddar cheese, grated*
- *Salt and pepper, to taste*
- *1 ham slice, cut into 2 pieces*
- *4 bread slices, flatten with a rolling pin*

Directions: Spray the inside of 2 ramekins with cooking spray.
Place 2 flat pieces of bread into each ramekin. Add the ham slice pieces into each ramekin.
Crack an egg in each ramekin, then sprinkle with cheese. Season with salt and pepper.
Place the ramekins into the air fryer at 300°F for 15 minutes. Serve warm.

Nutrition: Calories: 161.2, Fat: 7.8g, Carbs: 9.6g, Protein: 12.1g

Oriental Omelet

Preparation Time: 10 minutes
Cooking Time: 24 minutes
Servings: 1

Ingredients:

- *½ cup fresh Shimeji mushrooms, sliced*
- *2 eggs, whisked*
- *Salt and pepper, to taste*
- *1 clove garlic, minced*
- *A handful of sliced tofu*
- *2 tbsp. onion, finely chopped*
- *Cooking spray*

Directions: Spray the baking dish with cooking spray. Add onions and garlic. Air fry in the preheated air fryer at 355°F for 4 minutes. Place the tofu and mushrooms over the onions and add salt and pepper to taste.
Whisk the eggs and pour them over tofu and mushrooms. Air fry again for 20 minutes. Serve warm.

Nutrition: Calories: 209.5, Fat: 10.5g, Carbs: 8.4g, Protein: 12.9g

Crispy Breakfast Avocado Fries

Preparation Time: 10 minutes
Cooking Time: 6 minutes
Servings: 2

Ingredients:

- *2 eggs, beaten*
- *2 large avocados, peeled, pitted, cut into 8 slices each*
- *¼ tsp. pepper*
- *½ tsp. cayenne pepper*
- *Salt, to taste*
- *½ a lemon, Juice*
- *½ cup whole-wheat flour*
- *1 cup whole-wheat breadcrumbs*
- *Greek yogurt to serve*

Directions: Add flour, salt, pepper, and cayenne pepper to bowl and mix. Add bread crumbs into another bowl. Beat eggs in a third bowl.

First, dredge the avocado slices in the flour mixture. Next, dip them into the egg mixture, and finally dredge them in the breadcrumbs. Place avocado fries into the air fryer basket. Preheat the air fryer to 390°F.

Place the air fryer basket into the air fryer and cook for 6 minutes.

When Cooking Time is completed, transfer the avocado fries onto a serving platter. Sprinkle with lemon juice and serve with Greek yogurt.

Nutrition: Calories: 271.5, Fat: 12.9g, Carbs: 10.8g, Protein: 15.9g

Cheese and Egg Breakfast Sandwich

Preparation Time: 10 minutes
Cooking Time: 6 minutes
Servings: 1

Ingredients:

- *1–2 eggs*
- *1–2 slices cheddar or Swiss cheese*
- *A bit butters*
- *1 roll sliced in half (your choice, Kaiser Bun, English muffin, etc.)*

Directions: Butter your sliced roll on both sides.

Place the eggs in an oven-safe dish and whisk. Add seasoning if you wish, such as dill, chives, oregano, and salt.

Place the egg dish, roll, and cheese into the air fryer.

Make assured the buttered sides of the roll are in front of upwards. Set the air fryer to 390°F with a Cooking Time of 6 minutes. Remove the ingredients when Cooking Time is completed by the air fryer.

Place the egg and cheese between the pieces of roll and serve warm.

You might like to try adding slices of avocado and tomatoes to this breakfast sandwich!

Nutrition: Calories: 211.5, Fat: 10.7g, Carbs: 9.1g, Protein: 12.8g

Breakfast Cod Nuggets

Preparation Time: 10 minutes
Cooking Time: 10 minutes
Servings: 4

Ingredients:

- *1 lb. cod*

For breading:

- *2 eggs, beaten*
- *2 tbsp. olive oil*
- *1 cup almond flour*
- *¾ cup breadcrumbs*

- *1 tsp. dried parsley*
- *Pinch sea salt*
- *½ tsp. black pepper*

Directions: Preheat the air fryer to 390°F.

Cut the cod into strips about 1-inch by 2-inches. Blend breadcrumbs, olive oil, salt, parsley, and pepper in a food processor.

In 3 separate bowls, add breadcrumbs, eggs, and flour. Place each piece of fish into flour, then the eggs, and the breadcrumbs. Add pieces of cod to the air fryer basket and cook for 10 minutes. Serve warm.

Nutrition: Calories: 212.5, Fat: 12.2g, Carbs: 8.8g, Protein: 13.6g

Vegetable Egg Pancake

Preparation Time: 10 minutes
Cooking Time: 15 minutes
Servings: 2

Ingredients:

- *1 cup almond flour*
- *½ cup milk*
- *1 tbsp. parmesan cheese, grated*
- *3 eggs*
- *1 potato, grated*
- *1 beet, peeled and grated*
- *1 carrot, grated*
- *1 zucchini, grated*
- *1 tbsp. olive oil*
- *¼ tsp. nutmeg*
- *1 tsp. onion powder*
- *1 tsp. garlic powder*
- *½ tsp. black pepper*

Directions: Preheat your air fryer to 390°F.

Mix the zucchini, potato, beet, carrot, eggs, milk, almond flour, and parmesan in a bowl. Place olive oil into an oven-safe dish. Form patties with the vegetable mix and flatten them to form patties.

Place patties into an oven-safe dish and cook in the air fryer for 15 minutes.

Serve with sliced tomatoes, sour cream, and toast.

Nutrition: Calories: 222.8, Fat: 10.8g, Carbs: 10.1g, Proteins: 13.8g

Baked Mini Quiche

Preparation Time: 10 minutes
Cooking Time: 15 minutes
Servings: 2

Ingredients:

- *2 eggs*
- *1 large yellow onion, diced*
- *1 ¾ cups whole-wheat flour*
- *1 ½ cups spinach, chopped*
- *¾ cup cottage cheese*
- *Salt and black pepper, to taste*
- *2 tbsp. olive oil*
- *¾ cup butter*
- *¼ cup milk*

Directions: Preheat the air fryer to 355°F. Add the flour, butter, salt, and milk to the bowl and knead the dough until smooth and refrigerate for 15 minutes. Abode a frying pan over medium heat and add the oil to it.

When the oil is heated, add the onions into the pan and sauté them. Introduce spinach to the pan and cook until it wilts. Drain the excess moisture from spinach. Whisk the eggs together and add cheese to the bowl, and mix.

Take the dough out of the fridge and divide it into eight equal parts. Roll the dough into a ball that will fit into the bottom of the quiche mound. Place the rolled dough into molds. Place the spinach filling over the dough.

Place molds into air fryer basket and place basket inside of air fryer and cook for 15 minutes.

Remove quiche from molds and serve warm or cold.

Nutrition: Calories: 261.4, Fat: 7.8g, Carbs: 7.1g, Protein: 9.9g

Snacks and Appetizers

Air Fried Bacon-Wrapped Jalapeno Poppers

Preparation Time: 10 minutes
Cooking Time: 8 minutes
Servings: 10

Ingredients:

- *Cream cheese: 1/3 cup*
- *Ten jalapenos*
- *Bacon: 5 strips*

Directions: Let the air fryer preheat to 370 °F.
Wash and pat dry the jalapenos. Cut in half and take out the seeds. Spread the cream cheese.
Cut the bacon strips in half. Wrap the cream cheese filled jalapenos with slices of bacon.
Secure with a toothpick.
Place the jalapenos in the air fryer, cook at 370 °F for 6-8 minutes.

Nutrition: Calories: 74.7, Protein: 3.5g, Carbs: 1.4g, Fat: 6.3g

Crisp Egg Cups

Preparation Time: 10 minutes
Cooking Time: 10 minutes
Servings: 4

Ingredients:

- *Toasted whole-wheat bread: 4 slices*
- *Cooking spray*
- *4 eggs*
- *1 and a half tbsp. butter (trans-fat free)*
- *Ham: 1 thick slice*
- *Salt: 1/8 tsp*
- *Black pepper: 1/8 tsp*

Directions: Let the air fryer Preheat to 375 ° F. Take four ramekins, and spray with cooking spray.
Trim off the crusts from bread, and add butter to one side. Put the bread down into a ramekin, with butter-side in.
Cut the ham in strips, half-inch thick, and add on top of the bread.
Add one egg to each ramekin. Add salt and pepper.
Put the custard cups in the air fryer at 375 °F for 10–13 minutes.

Nutrition: Calories: 148.5, Protein: 11.5g, Carbs: 4.7g, Fat: 7.7g

Lemon-Garlic Tofu with Quinoa

Preparation Time: 20 minutes
Cooking Time: 15 minutes
Servings: 2

Ingredients:

- *Cooked quinoa: 2 cups*
- *Lemons: two zest and juice*
- *Sea salt & white pepper to taste*
- *Tofu: one block - pressed and sliced into half pieces*
- *Garlic – minced: 2 cloves*

Directions: Add the tofu into a deep dish.
In another bowl, add the garlic, lemon juice, lemon zest, salt, pepper.
Pour this marinade over tofu. Let it marinate for 15 minutes.
Add the tofu to the air fryer basket. Let it air fry at 370°F for 15 minutes. Shake the basket after 8 minutes of cooking. In a big deep bowl, add the cooked quinoa with the lemon-garlic Tofu, and serve.

Nutrition: Calories: 185.6, Protein: 21.5g, Carbs: 7.1g, Fat: 8.1g

Vegan Mashed Potato

Preparation Time: 10 minutes
Cooking Time: 10 minutes
Servings: 4

Ingredients:

For mashed potatoes:

- *Olive oil*
- *Red potatoes cooked with the skin on, cut into one-inch pieces*
- *1/4 tsp of salt*
- *Sea salt and black pepper - to taste*
- *Half cup of unsweetened soy milk or vegan milk*

For the Tofu:

- *One teaspoon of garlic powder*
- *One block of extra firm tofu: pressed, cut into one-inch pieces*
- *Light soy sauce:2 tablespoons*

Directions: Add the red cooked potatoes to a large bowl, mash with masher with olive oil. Then add milk and mix well.
Cover the bowl with plastic wrap, so it will keep warm and let it rest.
Meanwhile, add the tofu in one even layer in the air fryer, add the garlic and soy sauce, and make sure to cover all the tofu. Let it cook for ten minutes at 400°F. In the bowls, add the mashed potatoes, and cover with tofu.

Nutrition: Calories: 250.6, Protein: 19.5g, Carbs: 10.6g, Fat: 14.7g

Vegetable Rolls

Preparation Time: 10 minutes
Cooking Time: 8 minutes
Servings: 4

Ingredients:

- *Toasted sesame seeds*
- *2 carrots, grated*
- *Spring roll wrappers*
- *One egg white*
- *A dash gluten-free soy sauce*
- *Half cabbage, sliced*
- *Olive oil: 2 tbsp.*

Directions: In a pan over high flame heat, 2 tbsp. of oil and sauté the chopped vegetables. Add soy sauce, turn off the heat, and add toasted sesame seeds. Lay rolls on a surface and spread egg white with a brush.
Add some vegetable mix in the wrapper and fold.
Spray the rolls with oil spray and cook in the Air Fryer for 8 minutes at 380°F.

Nutrition: Calories: 125.4, Protein: 12.4g, Carbs: 7.6g, Fat: 14.6g

Air Fried Zucchini Chips

Preparation Time: 10 minutes
Cooking Time: 10 minutes
Servings: 2

Ingredients:

- *Parmesan Cheese: 3 Tbsp.*
- *Garlic Powder: 1/4 tsp*
- *Thin sliced zucchini: 1 Cup*
- *Corn Starch: 1/4 Cup*
- *Onion Powder: 1/4 tsp*
- *Salt: 1/4 tsp*
- *Whole wheat Bread Crumbs: 1/2 Cup*
- *Olive oil*

Directions: Let the Air Fryer preheat to 390 ° F.
In a food processor, blend into finer pieces garlic powder, salt, bread crumbs, parmesan cheese, and onion powder.

In 2 separate bowls, add corn starch in one, and whole wheat breadcrumb in the other.
Coat zucchini chips into corn starch, then coat in bread crumbs.
Spray the air fryer basket with olive oil. Add breaded zucchini chips in a single layer in the air fryer and spray with olive oil.
Air fry for six minutes at preheated temperature. Cook for another four minutes after turning zucchini chips.

Nutrition: Calories: 217.6, Protein: 12.4g, Carbs: 10.4g, Fat: 20.5g

Vegan Sandwich

Preparation Time: 10 minutes
Cooking Time: 10 minutes
Servings: 4

Ingredients:

For Tofu:

- *Garlic powder: 1 teaspoon*
- *Light soy sauce: 1/4 cup*
- *Turmeric: 1/2 teaspoon*
- *1 block extra firm pressed tofu: cut into 4 round slices*

For sandwich:

- *4 English vegan muffins*
- *Avocado: one cut into slices*
- *4 tomato slices*
- *Vegan cheese: 4 slices*
- *1 sliced onion*
- *Vegan mayonnaise*

Directions: In a deep dish, add the tofu circles with turmeric, soy sauce, and garlic powder. Let it for 10 minutes.
Put the marinated tofu in an air fryer. Cook for ten minutes at 400 ° F and shake the basket after 5 minutes.
Add vegan mayonnaise to the English muffins. Add vegan cheese, avocado slices, tomato, onion, and marinated, cooked tofu. Top with the other half of the muffins.

Nutrition: Calories: 196.7, Protein: 19.5g, Carbs: 11.6g, Fat: 8.7g

Air Fryer Ham Tarts

Preparation Time: 5 minutes
Cooking Time: 20 minutes
Servings: 4

Ingredients:

- *Chopped fresh chives: one tbsp.*
- *Frozen puff pastry: one sheet, thawed*
- *Eggs: four large*
- *4 tbsp. cooked ham, chopped*
- *4 tbsp. of Cheddar cheese, shredded*

Directions: Let the air fryer preheat to 400 °F. Lay puff pastry on a surface and slice into four squares.
Add two squares of puff pastry in the air fryer and cook for 8 minutes.
Take out from the air fryer and make an indentation in the dough's center. Add one tbsp. Of ham and one tbsp. of cheddar cheese in every hole. Add one egg to it. Add on the other two squares of pastry. Seal the dough seams with water and pinch.
Return the basket to the air fryer. Let it cook for about six minutes.
Take out from the basket of the air fryer and cool for 5 minutes.
Top with chives and serve hot.

Nutrition: Calories: 152.6, Protein: 10.4g, Carbs: 6.8g, Fat: 6.8g

Green Onions and Parmesan Tomatoes

Preparation Time: 7 minutes
Cooking Time: 15 minutes
Servings: 4

Ingredients:

- *4 large tomatoes, cut into slices*
- *1 tbsp. olive oil*
- *Salt and pepper to taste*
- *1/2 tsp. thyme, dried*
- *2 garlic cloves, minced*
- *2 green onions, finely chopped*
- *1/2 cup Parmesan cheese, freshly grated*

Directions: Preheat your air fryer to 390ºF.
Coat the tomato slices with olive oil and season with garlic, thyme, salt, and pepper.
Top with Parmesan and chopped green onions.
Place the tomatoes in the air fryer and cook for 15 minutes.
Serve on top of crostini or any meat, poultry, or fish.

Nutrition: Calories: 68.7, Fat: 3.3g, Carbs: 64.9g, Protein: 1.9g

Green Bell Peppers With Cauliflower Stuffing

Preparation Time: 7 minutes

Cooking Time: 10 minutes
Servings: 4

Ingredients:

- *4 green bell peppers, top cut, deseeded*
- *1 tsp. lemon juice*
- *2 tbsp. coriander leaves, finely chopped*
- *2 green chilies, finely chopped*
- *2 cups cauliflower, cooked and mashed*
- *2 onions, finely chopped*
- *1 tsp. cumin seeds*
- *1/4 tsp. turmeric powder*
- *1/4 tsp. chili powder*
- *1/4 tsp. garam masala*
- *Salt to taste*
- *Olive oil as needed*

Directions: In a saucepan, warm the oil and sauté the chilies, onion, and cumin seeds. Swell the rest of the ingredients except the bell peppers and mix well.
Preheat the air fryer to 390ºF for 10 minutes.
Brush the green bell peppers with olive oil inside and out and stuff each pepper with cauliflower mixture.
Place them into the air fryer and grill for 10 minutes.

Nutrition: Calories: 256.8, Fat: 3.7g, Carbs: 44.1g, Protein: 12.7g

Crispy Potatoes

Preparation Time: 10 minutes
Cooking Time: 15 minutes
Servings: 3

Ingredients:

- *Red potatoes: 1 and 1/2 pounds*
- *Aquafaba: 1 tablespoon*
- *Tomato paste: 1 teaspoon*
- *Sea salt: 1 teaspoon*
- *Brown rice flour: half tablespoon*
- *Garlic powder: half teaspoon*
- *Sweet smoked paprika: 3/4 tsp.*

Directions: Cut the potatoes into small quarters, making sure they are the same sized. The maximum thickness of potatoes should be one and a half-inch thick.
Boil the potatoes, drain and add them in a large bowl. In another bowl, add tomato paste and aquafaba.
In a third bowl, mix the remaining ingredients with flour.

Now add the last two bowls to the potatoes, and coat every piece.
Preheat the air fryer to 360°F for 3 minutes, then place the potatoes in the basket and cook for 12 minutes.
Shake the basket every six minutes, making sure no potatoes get stuck on the bottom.

Nutrition: Calories: 170.5, Protein: 5.5g, Carbs: 21.6g, Fat: 4.8g

Veggie Air Fryer Eggs

Preparation Time: 10 minutes
Cooking Time: 14 minutes
Servings: 4

Ingredients:

- *Shredded cheese: 1 cup*
- *Non-stick cooking spray*
- *Vegetables of your choice: 1 cup diced*
- *Chopped cilantro: 1 Tbsp.*
- *Four eggs*
- *Salt and Pepper to taste*

Directions: Take four ramekins, grease them with oil.
In a bowl, crack the eggs with half the cheese, cilantro, salt, diced vegetables, and pepper. Pour in the ramekins.
Put in the air-fryer basket and cook for 12 minutes, at 300 ° F. Then add the cheese to the cups.
Set the air-fryer at 400 degrees F and continue to cook for two minutes, until cheese is lightly browned and melted.

Nutrition: Calories: 193.7, Protein: 15.5g, Carbs: 6.1g, Fat: 10.5g

Cheesy Chickpea and Zucchini Burgers

Preparation Time: 7 minutes
Cooking Time: 15 minutes
Servings: 4

Ingredients:

- *1 can chickpeas, drained*
- *3 tbsp. coriander*
- *1 oz. cheddar cheese, shredded*
- *2 eggs, beaten*
- *1 tsp. garlic puree*
- *1 zucchini spiralized*
- *1 red onion, diced*
- *1 tsp. chili powder*

- *1 tsp. mixed spice*
- *Salt and pepper to taste*
- *1 tsp. cumin*

Directions: Mix all the ingredients in a mixing bowl.
Shape portions of the mixture into burgers. Place in the air fryer at 300ºF for 15 minutes.

Nutrition: Calories: 184.1, Fat: 9.7g, Carbs: 18.1g, Protein: 12.8g

Spicy Sweet Potatoes

Preparation Time: 7 minutes
Cooking Time: 23 minutes
Servings: 4

Ingredients:

- *3 sweet potatoes, peeled and chopped into chips*
- *1 tsp. chili powder*
- *1 tsp. paprika*
- *2 tbsp. olive oil*
- *1 tbsp. red wine vinegar*
- *1 tomato, thinly sliced*
- *1/2 cup tomato sauce*
- *1 onion, peeled and diced*
- *Salt and pepper to taste*
- *1 tsp. rosemary*
- *1 tsp. oregano*
- *1 tsp. mixed spice*
- *2 tsp. thyme*
- *2 tsp. coriander*

Directions: Toss the chips in a bowl with olive oil. Add to the air fryer and cook for 15 minutes at 360ºF.
Mix the remaining ingredients in a baking dish. Place the sauce in the air fryer for 8 minutes.
Toss the potatoes in the sauce and serve warmly.

Nutrition: Calories: 302.5, Fat: 4.6g, Carbs: 56.5g, Protein: 8.7g

Parmesan Cauliflower

Preparation Time: 12 minutes
Cooking Time: 20 minutes
Servings: 20 cauliflower bites

Ingredients:

- *4 cups cauliflower florets*
- *1 cup whole-wheat bread crumbs*
- *1 tsp. coarse sea salt or kosher salt*
- *1/4 cup Parmesan cheese, grated*
- *1/4 cup butter*
- *1/4 cup mild hot sauce*
- *Olive oil spray*

Directions: Place a parchment liner in the air fryer basket.
Cut the cauliflower florets in half and set them aside.
In a small bowl, mix the bread crumbs, salt, and Parmesan; set aside.
In a small microwave-safe bowl, combine the hot sauce and butter. Heat in the microwave until the butter is melted, about 15 seconds. Whisk.
Holding the stems of the cauliflower florets, dip them in the butter mixture to coat. Shake off any excess mixture.
Dredge the dipped florets with the bread crumb mixture, then put them in the air fryer basket. There's no need for a single layer; just toss them all in there.
Spray the cauliflower lightly with olive oil and air fry at 350ºF for 15 minutes, shaking the basket a few times throughout the cooking process. The florets are done when they are lightly browned and crispy. Serve warm.

Nutrition: Calories: 105.5, Fat: 5.7g, Protein: 3.5g, Carbs: 9.5g, Fiber: 1g, Sugar: 1g

Cream Buns with Strawberries

Preparation Time: 10 minutes
Cooking Time: 12 minutes
Servings: 6

Ingredients:
- *240g all-purpose flour*
- *50g granulated sugar*
- *8g baking powder*
- *1g of salt*
- *85g chopped cold butter*
- *84g chopped fresh strawberries*
- *120 ml whipping cream*
- *2 large eggs*
- *10 ml vanilla extract*
- *5 ml of water*

Directions: Sift flour, sugar, baking powder and salt in a large bowl. Put the butter with the flour with the use of a blender or your hands until the mixture resembles thick crumbs.

Mix the strawberries in the flour mixture. Set aside for the mixture to stand. Beat the whipping cream, 1 egg and the vanilla extract in a separate bowl.

Put the cream mixture in the flour mixture until they are homogeneous, and then spread the mixture to a thickness of 38 mm.

Use a round cookie cutter to cut the buns. Spread the buns with a combination of egg and water. Set aside

Preheat the air fryer, set it to 375°F.

Place baking paper in the preheated inner basket. Place the buns on top and cook for 12 minutes.

Nutrition: Calories: 149, Fat: 13.4g, Carbs: 2.8g, Protein: 11.2g, Sugar: 7.6g

Blueberry Buns

Preparation Time: 10 minutes
Cooking Time: 12 minutes
Servings: 6

Ingredients:

- *240g all-purpose flour*
- *50g granulated sugar*
- *8g baking powder*
- *2g of salt*
- *85g chopped cold butter*
- *85g of fresh blueberries*
- *3g grated fresh ginger*
- *113 ml whipping cream*
- *2 large eggs*
- *4 ml vanilla extract*
- *5 ml of water*

Directions: Put sugar, flour, baking powder and salt in a large bowl.

Put the butter with the flour using a blender or your hands until the mixture resembles thick crumbs.

Mix the blueberries and ginger in the flour mixture and set aside.

Mix the whipping cream, 1 egg and the vanilla extract in a different container.

Put the cream mixture with the flour mixture until combined.

Shape the dough until it reaches a thickness of approximately 38 mm and cut it into eighths.

Spread the buns with a combination of egg and water. Set aside Preheat the air fryer set it to 380°F.

Place baking paper in the preheated inner basket and place the buns on top of the paper. Cook for 12 minutes.

Nutrition: Calories: 104, Fat: 1.63g, Carbs: 19.3g, Protein: 2.4g, Sugar: 2g

Red Cabbage and Mushroom Stickers

Preparation Time: 12 minutes
Cooking Time: 15 minutes
Servings: 12 potstickers

Ingredients:

- *1 cup red cabbage, shredded*
- *1/4 cup button mushrooms, chopped*
- *1/4 cup carrot, grated*
- *2 tbsp. onion, minced*
- *2 garlic cloves, minced*
- *2 tsp. fresh ginger, grated*
- *12 Gyoza potsticker wrappers*
- *2 1/2 tsp. olive oil, divided*
- *1 tbsp. water*

Directions: Combine the red cabbage, mushrooms, carrot, onion, garlic, and ginger in a baking pan. Add 1 tbsp. of water. Place in the air fryer and bake at 370ºF for 6 minutes, until the vegetables are crisp-tender. Drain and set aside.
Working one at a time, place the potsticker wrappers on a work surface. Top each wrapper with a scant 1 tbsp. of the filling. Fold half of the wrapper over the other half to form a half-circle. Dab with water and press both edges together.
Spread 1 1/4 tsp. of olive oil on the baking pan. Put half of the potstickers, seam-side up, in the pan. Air fry for 5 minutes. Add 1 tbsp. of water and return the pan to the air fryer.
Air fry for 4 minutes more, or until hot. Repeat with the remaining potstickers, the remaining 1 1/4 tsp. of oil, and another tbsp. of water. Serve immediately.

Nutrition: Calories: 87.5, Fat: 2.8g, Protein: 2.5g, Carbs: 13.5g, Fiber: 1g, Sugar: 1g

Onion Bites

Preparation Time: 10 minutes
Cooking Time: 10 minutes
Servings: 20 onion bites

Ingredients:

- *20 white boiler onions*
- *1 cup buttermilk*
- *2 eggs*
- *1 cup flour*
- *1 cup whole-wheat bread crumbs*
- *1 tbsp. smoked paprika*

- *1 tsp. salt*
- *1 tsp. ground black pepper*
- *1 tsp. garlic, granulated*
- *3/4 tsp. chili powder*
- *Olive oil spray*

Directions: Place a parchment liner in the air fryer basket.

Slice off the root end of the onions, taking off as little as possible.

Peel off the papery skin and make cuts halfway through the tops of the onions. Don't cut too far down; you want the onion to hold together still. In a large bowl, beat the buttermilk and eggs together.

Mix the flour, bread crumbs, paprika, salt, pepper, garlic, and chili powder in a medium bowl.

Add the prepared onions to the buttermilk mixture and allow to soak for at least 10 minutes.

Remove the onions from the batter and dredge them with the bread crumb mixture.

Place the prepared onions in the air fryer basket in a single layer. Spray lightly with olive oil and air fry at 360ºF for 8–10 minutes, until golden and crispy. Repeat with any remaining onions and serve.

Nutrition: Calories: 165.5, Fat: 1.8g, Protein: 6.4g, Carbs: 30.5g, Fiber: 4g, Sugar: 6.7g

French Toast in Sticks

Preparation Time: 5 minutes
Cooking Time: 10 minutes
Servings: 4

Ingredients:

- *4 slices of white bread, 38 mm thick, preferably hard*
- *2 eggs*
- *60 ml of milk*
- *15 ml maple sauce*
- *2 ml vanilla extract*
- *Nonstick Spray Oil*
- *38g of sugar*
- *3ground cinnamon*
- *Maple syrup, to serve*
- *Sugar to sprinkle*

Directions: Cut each slice of bread into thirds making 12 pieces. Place sideways.

Beat the eggs, milk, maple syrup and vanilla.

Preheat the air fryer, to 330°F.

Dip the sliced   bread in the egg mixture and place it in the preheated air fryer. Sprinkle French toast generously with oil spray. Cook French toast for 10 minutes at 330°F. Turn the toast halfway through cooking.
Mix the sugar and cinnamon in a bowl. Cover the French toast with the sugar and cinnamon mixture when you have finished cooking.
Serve with Maple syrup and sprinkle with powdered sugar.

Nutrition: Calories 126, Fat 5.2g, Carbs 16.1g, Sugar 3.2g, Protein 3.1g

Poultry

Lemon-Garlic Chicken

Preparation Time: 2 hours
Cooking Time: 35 minutes
Servings: 4

Ingredients:

- *Lemon juice ¼ cup*
- *1 Tbsp. olive oil*
- *1 tsp mustard*
- *Cloves of garlic*
- *¼ tsp salt*
- *⅛ tsp black pepper*
- *Chicken thighs*
- *Lemon wedges*

Directions: In a bowl, whisk together the olive oil, lemon juice, mustard Dijon, garlic, salt, and pepper.

Place the chicken thighs in a large ziploc bag. Spill marinade over chicken & seal bag, ensuring all chicken parts are covered. Cool for at least 2 hours.

Preheat a frying pan to 360 F. Remove the chicken with towels from the marinade, & pat dry.

Place pieces of chicken in the air fryer basket, if necessary, cook them in batches.

Fry till chicken is no longer pink on the bone & the juices run smoothly, 22 to 24 min. Upon serving, press a lemon slice across each piece.

Nutrition: Calories: 257.5, Protein: 19.9g, Carbs: 3.1g, Fat: 18.1g

Chicken Pie

Preparation Time: 10 minutes
Cooking Time: 30 minutes
Servings: 2

Ingredients:

- *Puff pastry: 2 sheets*
- *Chicken thighs: 2 pieces, cut into cubes*
- *One small onion, chopped*
- *Small potatoes: 2, chopped*
- *Mushrooms: 1/4 cup*
- *Light soya sauce*
- *One carrot, chopped*
- *Black pepper to taste*
- *Worcestershire sauce: to taste*
- *Salt to taste*
- *Italian mixed dried herbs*

- *Garlic powder: a pinch*
- *Plain flour: 2 tbsp.*
- *Milk, as required*
- *Melted butter*

Directions: In a mixing bowl, add light soya sauce and pepper add the chicken cubes, and coat well.

In a pan over medium heat, sauté potatoes, carrot, and onion. Add some water, if required, to cook the vegetables. Add the chicken cubes and mushrooms and cook them too.

Stir in black pepper, salt, Worcestershire sauce, garlic powder, and dried herbs.

When the chicken is cooked through, add some of the flour and mix well.

Add in the milk and let the vegetables simmer until tender.

Place one piece of puff pastry in the baking tray of the air fryer, poke holes with a fork.

Add on top the cooked chicken filling and eggs and puff pastry on top with holes. Cut the excess pastry off. Glaze with melted butter.

Air fry at 180 F for six minutes, or until it becomes golden brown.

Serve right away and enjoy.

Nutrition: Calories: 223.5, Protein: 20.5g, Carbs: 16.4g, Fat: 17.5 g

Blackened Chicken Breast

Preparation Time: 10 minutes
Cooking Time: 20 minutes
Servings: 2

Ingredients:

- *Paprika: 2 teaspoons*
- *Ground thyme: 1 teaspoon*
- *Cumin: 1 teaspoon*
- *Cayenne pepper: half tsp.*
- *Onion powder: half tsp.*
- *Black Pepper: half tsp.*
- *Salt: ¼ teaspoon*
- *Vegetable oil: 2 teaspoons*
- *Pieces of chicken breast halves (without bones and skin)*

Directions: In a mixing bowl, add onion powder, salt, cumin, paprika, black pepper, thyme, and cayenne pepper. Mix it well.

Drizzle oil over chicken and rub. Dip each piece of chicken in blackening spice blend on both sides.

Let it rest for five minutes while the air fryer is preheating. Preheat it for five minutes at 360°F.

Put the chicken in the air fryer and let it cook for ten minutes. Flip and then cook for another ten minutes.

After, let it sit for five minutes, then slice and serve with the side of greens.

Nutrition: Calories: 431.4, Protein: 79.8g, Carbs: 2.8g, Fat: 9.1g

Herb-Marinated Chicken Thighs

Preparation Time: 30 minutes
Cooking Time: 12 minutes
Servings: 4

Ingredients:

- *Chicken thighs: 8 skin-on, bone-in,*
- *Lemon juice: 2 Tablespoon*
- *Onion powder: half teaspoon*
- *Garlic powder: 2 teaspoon*
- *Spike Seasoning: 1 teaspoon.*
- *Olive oil: 1/4 cup*
- *Dried basil: 1 teaspoon*
- *Dried oregano: half teaspoon.*
- *Black Pepper: 1/4 tsp*

Directions: In a bowl, add dried oregano, olive oil, lemon juice, dried sage, garlic powder, Spike Seasoning, onion powder, dried basil, black pepper.
In a ziploc bag, add the spice blend and the chicken and mix well. Marinate the chicken in the refrigerator for six hours or more.
Preheat the air fryer to 360F.
Put the chicken in the air fryer basket, cook for 6 minutes, flip the chicken, and cook for 6 minutes more.
Take out from the air fryer and serve with microgreens.

Nutrition: Calories: 99.6, Protein: 4.5g, Carbs: 1g, Fat: 8.7g

Popcorn Chicken in Air Fryer

Preparation Time: 10 minutes
Cooking Time: 10 minutes
Servings: 4

Ingredients:
For Marinade:

- *8 cups, chicken tenders, cut into bite-size pieces*
- *Freshly ground black pepper: 1/2 tsp*
- *Almond milk: 2 cups*
- *Salt: 1 tsp*
- *Paprika: 1/2 tsp*

Dry Mix:

- *Salt: 3 tsp*
- *Flour: 3 cups*
- *Paprika: 2 tsp*
- *Oil spray*
- *Freshly ground black pepper: 2 tsp*

Directions: In a bowl, add all marinade ingredients and chicken. Mix well, and put it in a ziploc bag and refrigerator for two hours for the minimum, or six hours.
In a large bowl, add all the dry ingredients.
Coat the marinated chicken to the dry mix. Into the marinade again, then for the second time in the dry mixture.
Spray the air fryer basket with olive oil and place the breaded chicken pieces in one single layer. Spray oil over the chicken pieces too. Cook at 370F for 10 minutes, tossing halfway through.
Serve immediately with salad greens or dipping sauce.

Nutrition: Calories: 339.5, Protein: 20.5g, Carbs: 13.4g, Fat: 9.6g

Air Fryer Brown Rice Chicken Fried

Preparation Time: 10 minutes
Cooking Time: 10 minutes
Servings: 2

Ingredients:

- *Olive Oil Cooking Spray*
- *Chicken Breast: 1 Cup, Diced & Cooked &*
- *White Onion: 1/4 cup chopped*
- *Celery: 1/4 Cup chopped*
- *Cooked brown rice: 4 Cups*
- *Carrots: 1/4 cup chopped*

Directions: Place foil on the air fryer basket, make sure to leave room for air to flow, roll up on the sides.
Spray with olive oil. Mix all ingredients and add them on the top of the foil, in the air fryer basket.
Give an olive oil spray on the mixture. Cook for five minutes at 390°F.
Open the air fryer and give a toss to the mixture. Cook for five more minutes at 390F.

Nutrition: Calories: 349.6, Protein: 22.4g, Carbs: 19.8g, Fat: 5.6g

Chicken with Mixed Vegetables

Preparation Time: 10 minutes

Cooking Time: 10 minutes
Servings: 2

Ingredients:

- *1/2 onion diced*
- *Chicken breast: 4 cups, cubed pieces*
- *Half zucchini chopped*
- *Italian seasoning: 1 tablespoon*
- *Bell pepper chopped: 1/2 cup*
- *Clove of garlic pressed*
- *Broccoli florets: 1/2 cup*
- *Olive oil: 2 tablespoons*
- *Half teaspoon of chili powder, garlic powder, pepper, salt*

Directions: Let the air fryer heat to 400 F and dice the vegetables.
In a bowl, add the seasoning, oil and add vegetables, chicken and toss well.
Place chicken and vegetables in the air fryer, and cook for ten minutes, toss half way through, cook in batches.
Make sure the veggies are charred and the chicken is cooked through.
Serve hot.

Nutrition: Calories: 229.6, Protein: 26.5g, Carbs: 7.6g, Fat: 9.5g

Garlic Parmesan Chicken Tenders

Preparation Time: 5 minutes
Cooking Time: 12 minutes
Servings: 4

Ingredients:

- *One egg*
- *Eight raw chicken tenders*
- *Water: 2 tablespoons*
- *Olive oil*

To coat:

- *Panko breadcrumbs: 1 cup*
- *Half tsp of salt*
- *Black Pepper: 1/4 teaspoon*
- *Garlic powder: 1 teaspoon*
- *Onion powder: 1/2 teaspoon*
- *Parmesan cheese: 1/4 cup*
- *Any dipping Sauce*

Directions: Add all the coating ingredients in a big bowl.

In another bowl, mix water and egg. Dip the chicken in the egg mix, then in the coating mix.
Put the tenders in the air fry basket in a single layer. Spray with the olive oil.
Cook at 400 degrees for 12 minutes. Flip the chicken halfway through.

Nutrition: Calories: 219.6, Protein: 27.6g, Carbs: 12.5g, Fat: 5.6g

Buttermilk Chicken in Air-Fryer

Preparation Time: 30 minutes
Cooking Time: 20 minutes
Servings: 6

Ingredients:

- *Chicken thighs: 4 cups skin-on, bone-in*

Marinade:

- *Buttermilk: 2 cups*
- *Black pepper: 2 tsp.*
- *Cayenne pepper: 1 tsp.*
- *Salt: 2 tsp.*

Seasoned Flour:

- *Baking powder: 1 tbsp.*
- *All-purpose flour: 2 cups*
- *Paprika powder: 1 tbsp.*
- *Salt: 1 tsp.*
- *Garlic powder: 1 tbsp.*

Directions: Let the air fry heat at 356F. With a paper towel, pat dry the chicken thighs.
In a mixing bowl, add paprika, black pepper, salt mix well, then add chicken pieces. Add
buttermilk and coat the chicken well. Let it marinate for at least 6 hours.
In another bowl, add baking powder, salt, flour, pepper, and paprika. Put one by one of the
chicken pieces and coat in the seasoning mix.
Spray oil on chicken pieces and place breaded chicken skin side up in air fryer basket in
one layer, cook for 8 minutes, then flip the chicken pieces' cook for another ten minutes.

Nutrition: Calories: 209.6, Protein: 22.5g, Carbs: 11.8g, Fat: 17.5 g

Chicken Bites in Air Fryer

Preparation Time: 10 minutes
Cooking Time: 8 minutes
Servings: 3

Ingredients:

- *Chicken breast: 2 cups*

- *Kosher salt& pepper to taste*
- *Smashed potatoes: one cup*
- *Scallions: ¼ cup*
- *One Egg beat*
- *Whole wheat breadcrumbs:*
- *1 cup*

Directions: Boil the chicken until soft. Shred the chicken with the help of a fork. Add the smashed potatoes, scallions to the shredded chicken. Season with kosher salt and pepper. Coat with egg and then in bread crumbs.
Put in the air fryer, and cook for 8 minutes at 380F.
Serve warm.

Nutrition: Calories: 233.6, Protein: 25.6g, Carbs: 14.7g, Fat: 8.7 g

Brine-Soaked Turkey

Preparation Time: 10 minutes
Cooking Time: 45 minutes
Servings: 8

Ingredients
- *7 lbs. turkey breast, bone-in, skin-on*

For the brine
- *1/2 cup salt*
- *1 lemon*
- *1/2 onion*
- *3 garlic cloves, smashed*
- *5 sprigs fresh thyme*
- *3 bay leaves*
- *Black pepper*

For the turkey breast
- *4 tbsp. butter, softened*
- *1/2 tsp. black pepper*
- *1/2 tsp. garlic powder*
- *1/4 tsp. thyme, dried*
- *1/4 tsp. oregano, dried*

Directions: Mix the turkey brine ingredients in a pot and soak the turkey in the brine overnight. The next day, remove the soaked turkey from the brine.
Whisk the butter, black pepper, garlic powder, oregano, and thyme. Brush the butter mixture over the turkey, then place it in a baking tray.

Press the POWER button of the air fry oven and turn the dial to select the AIR ROAST mode.
Press the TIME button and again turn the dial to set the Cooking Time to 45 minutes.
Now push the TEMP button and rotate the dial to set the temperature at 370°F. Once preheated, place the turkey baking tray in the oven and close the lid.
Slice and serve warm.

Nutrition: Calories: 396.5, Carbs: 58.9g, Fat: 15.6g, Protein: 8.5g

Zucchini Turkey Burgers

Preparation Time: 10 minutes
Cooking Time: 10 minutes
Servings: 5

Ingredients:

- *Gluten-free breadcrumbs: 1/4 cup (seasoned)*
- *Grated zucchini: 1 cup*
- *Red onion: 1 tbsp. (grated)*
- *Lean ground turkey: 4 cups*
- *One clove of minced garlic*
- *1 tsp of kosher salt and fresh pepper*

Directions: In a bowl, add zucchini (moisture removed with a paper towel), ground turkey, garlic, salt, onion, pepper, breadcrumbs. Mix well. With your hands make five patties. But not too thick.
Let the air fryer preheat to 375 F.
Put in an air fryer in a single layer and cook for 7 minutes or more. Until cooked through and browned.
Place in buns with ketchup and lettuce and enjoy.

Nutrition: Calories: 160.6, Carbs: 4.1g, Protein: 18.6g, Fat: 6.5g

No-breaded Turkey Breast

Preparation Time: 5 minutes
Cooking Time: 40-60 minutes
Servings: 10

Ingredients:

- *Turkey breast: 4 pounds, ribs removed, bone with skin*
- *Olive oil: 1 tablespoon*
- *Salt: 2 teaspoons*
- *Dry turkey seasoning (without salt): half tsp.*

Directions: Rub half tbsp of olive oil over turkey breast. Sprinkle salt, turkey seasoning on both sides of turkey breast with half tbsp of olive oil.

Let the air fryer preheat at 350 F. put turkey skin side down in air fryer and cook for 20 minutes until the turkey's temperature reaches 160 F for half an hour to 40 minutes.

Let it sit for ten minutes before slicing.

Nutrition: Calories: 225.6, Carbs: 21.5g, Protein: 32.9g, Fat: 9.5g

Turkey Fajitas Platter in Air Fryer

Preparation Time: 5 minutes
Cooking Time: 20 minutes
Servings: 2

Ingredients:

- *Cooked Turkey Breast: 1/4 cup*
- *Six Tortilla Wraps*
- *One Avocado*
- *One Yellow Pepper*
- *One Red Pepper*
- *Half Red Onion*
- *Soft Cheese: 5 Tbsp.*
- *Mexican Seasoning: 2 Tbsp.*
- *Cumin: 1 Tsp*
- *Kosher salt& Pepper*
- *Cajun Spice: 3 Tbsp.*
- *Fresh Coriander*

Directions: Chop up the avocado and slice the vegetables.

Dice up turkey breast into small bite-size pieces.

In a bowl, add onions, turkey, soft cheese, and peppers along with seasonings. Mix it well.

Place it in foil and the air fryer. Cook for 20 minutes at 392 °F.

Serve hot.

Nutritional: Calories: 378.7, Protein: 30.6g, Carbs: 63.8g, Fat: 28.7g

Turkey Breast with Mustard Glaze

Preparation Time: 10 minutes
Cooking Time: 50 minutes
Servings: 6

Ingredients:

- *Whole turkey breast: 5 pounds*
- *Olive oil: 2 tsp.*
- *Dried sage: half tsp.*

- *Smoked paprika: half tsp.*
- *Dried thyme: one tsp.*
- *Salt: one tsp.*
- *Freshly ground black pepper: half tsp.*
- *Dijon mustard: 2 tbsp*

Directions: Let the air fryer preheat to 350 ° F. Rub the olive oil all over the turkey breast. In a bowl, mix salt, sage, pepper, thyme, and paprika. Mix well and coat turkey in this spice rub.

Place the turkey in an air fryer, cook for 25 minutes at 350ºF. Flip the turkey over and cook for another 12 minutes. Flip again and cook for another ten minutes. With an instant-read thermometer, the internal temperature should reach 165ºF.

In the meantime, in a saucepan, mix mustard and with one tsp. of butter.

Brush this glaze all over the turkey when cooked. Cook again for five minutes.

Nutritional: Calories: 378.6, Carbs: 20.5g, Protein: 52.7g, Fat: 22.6g

Parmesan Chicken Meatballs

Preparation Time: 10 minutes
Cooking Time: 12 minutes
Servings: 20

Ingredients:
- *Pork rinds: half cup, ground*
- *Ground chicken: 4 cups*
- *Parmesan cheese: half cup grated*
- *Kosher salt: 1 tsp.*
- *Garlic powder: 1/2 tsp.*
- *One egg beaten*
- *Paprika: 1/2 tsp.*
- *Pepper: half tsp.*
- *Whole wheat breadcrumbs: half cup ground*

Directions: Let the Air Fryer pre-heat to 400°F.

Add cheese, chicken, egg, pepper, half cup of pork rinds, garlic, salt, and paprika in a big mixing ball. Mix well into a dough, make into 1and half-inch balls.

Coat the meatballs in whole wheat bread crumbs.

Spray the oil in the air fry basket and add meatballs in one even layer.

Let it cook for 12 minutes at 400°F, flipping once halfway through. Serve with salad greens.

Nutrition: Calories: 239.5, Protein: 20.5g, Carbs: 11.5g, Fat: 9.6g

Air Fried Maple Chicken Thighs

Preparation Time: 10 minutes
Cooking Time: 25 minutes
Servings: 4

Ingredients:

- *One egg*
- *Buttermilk: 1 cup*
- *Maple syrup: half cup*
- *Chicken thighs: 4 pieces*
- *Granulated garlic: 1 tsp.*

Dry Mix:

- *Granulated garlic: half tsp.*
- *All-purpose flour: half cup*
- *Salt: one tbsp.*
- *Sweet paprika: one tsp.*
- *Smoked paprika: half tsp.*
- *Tapioca flour: ¼ cup*
- *Cayenne pepper: ¼ teaspoon*
- *Granulated onion: one tsp.*
- *Black pepper: ¼ teaspoon*
- *Honey powder: half tsp.*

Directions: In a ziploc bag, add egg, one tsp. of granulated garlic, buttermilk, and maple syrup, add in the chicken thighs and let it marinate for one hour or more in the refrigerator. In a mixing bowl, add sweet paprika, tapioca flour, granulated onion, half tsp. of granulated garlic, flour, cayenne pepper, salt, pepper, honey powder, and smoked paprika mix it well. Let the air fry preheat to 380 F. Coat the marinated chicken thighs in the dry spice mix, shake the excess off.
Put the chicken skin side down in the air fryer.
Let it cook for 12 minutes. Flip thighs halfway through and cook for 13 minutes more.

Nutrition: Calories: 415, Protein: 23.8g, Carbs: 20.1g, Fat: 12.8g

Mushroom Oatmeal

Preparation Time: 10 minutes
Cooking Time: 25 minutes
Servings: 4

Ingredients:

- *One small yellow onion, chopped*
- *1 cup steel-cut oats*
- *1 Garlic cloves, minced*
- *2 Tablespoons butter*

- *½ cup of water*
- *One and a half cup of canned chicken stock*
- *Thyme springs, chopped*
- *2 Tablespoons extra virgin olive oil*
- *½ cup gouda cheese, grated*
- *1 cup mushroom, sliced*
- *Salt and black pepper to taste*

Directions: Heat a pan over medium heat, which suits your air fryer with the butter, add onions and garlic, stir and cook for 4 minutes.

Add oats, sugar, salt, pepper, stock, and thyme, stir, place in the air fryer and cook for 16 minutes at 360 F.

In the meantime, prepare a skillet over medium heat with the olive oil, add mushrooms, cook them for 3 minutes, add oatmeal and cheese, whisk, divide into bowls and serve for breakfast.

Nutrition: Calories: 283.7, Protein: 17.5g, Carbs: 19.6g, Fat: 7.5g

Air Fryer Chicken & Broccoli

Preparation Time: 10 minutes
Cooking Time: 25 minutes
Servings: 4

Ingredients:

- *Olive oil: 2 Tablespoons*
- *Chicken breast: 4 cups, bone and skinless (cut into cubes)*
- *Half medium onion, roughly sliced*
- *Low sodium soy sauce: 1 Tbsp.*
- *Garlic powder: half teaspoon*
- *Rice vinegar: 2 teaspoons*
- *Broccoli: 1-2 cups, cut into florets*
- *Hot sauce: 2 teaspoons*
- *Fresh minced ginger: 1 Tbsp.*
- *Sesame seed oil: 1 teaspoon*
- *Salt & black pepper, to taste*

Directions: In a bowl, add chicken breast, onion, and broccoli. Combine them well.

In another bowl, add ginger, oil, sesame oil, rice vinegar, hot sauce, garlic powder, and soy sauce mix it well. Then add the broccoli, chicken, and onions to marinade.

Coat well the chicken with sauces. And let it rest in the refrigerator for 15 minutes.

Place chicken mix in one even layer in air fryer basket and cook for 16-20 minutes, at 380 F. halfway through, toss the basket and cook the chicken evenly.

Add five minutes more, if required. Add salt and pepper, if needed. Serve hot with lemon wedges.

Nutrition: Calories: 190.6, Protein: 25.6g, Carbs: 3.6g, Fat: 6.4g

No-Breading Chicken Breast in Air Fryer

Preparation Time: 10 minutes
Cooking Time: 10 minutes
Servings: 2

Ingredients:

- *Olive oil spray*
- *Chicken breasts: 4 (boneless)*
- *Onion powder: 3/4 teaspoon*
- *Salt: ¼ cup*
- *Smoked paprika: half tsp.*
- *1/8 tsp. of cayenne pepper*
- *Garlic powder: 3/4 teaspoon*
- *Dried parsley: half tsp.*

Directions: In a large bowl, add six cups of warm water, add salt (1/4 cup) and mix to dissolve.
Put chicken breasts in the warm salted water and let it refrigerate for almost 2 hours. Remove from water and pat dry.
In a bowl, add all the spices with ¾ tsp. of salt. Spray the oil all over the chicken and rub the spice mix all over the chicken.
Let the air fryer heat at 380F.
Put the chicken in the air fryer and cook for ten minutes. Flip halfway through and serve with salad green.

Nutrition: Calories: 207.5, Protein: 39.4g, Carbs: 1g, Fat: 4g

Red Meat

Lean Lamb and Turkey Meatballs with Yogurt

Preparation Time: 10 minutes
Cooking Time: 8 minutes
Servings: 4

Ingredients:

- *1 egg white*
- *4 oz. ground lean turkey*
- *1 lb. of lean ground lamb*
- *1 tsp. both cayenne pepper, ground coriander, red chili pastes, salt, and ground cumin*
- *2 garlic cloves, minced*
- *1 ½ tbsp. parsley, chopped*
- *1 tbsp. mint, chopped*
- *¼ cup of olive oil*

For the yogurt:

- *2 tbsp. of buttermilk*
- *1 garlic clove, minced*
- *¼ cup mint, chopped*
- *½ cup Greek yogurt, non-fat*
- *Salt, to taste*

Directions: Set the Air Fryer to 390°F.
Blend all the ingredients for the meatballs in a bowl. Roll and mound them into golf-size round pieces. Arrange in the cooking basket. Cook for 8 minutes.
Meantime, combine all the ingredients for the mint yogurt in a bowl. Mix well.
Serve the meatballs with mint yogurt. Top with olives and fresh mint.

Nutrition: Calories: 154 Carbs: 9 g Fat: 2.5 g Protein: 8.6 g Fiber: 2.4 g

Air Fried Empanadas

Preparation Time: 10 minutes
Cooking Time: 20 minutes
Servings: 2

Ingredients:

- *Square gyoza wrappers: eight pieces*
- *Olive oil: 1 tablespoon*
- *White onion: 1/4 cup, finely diced*
- *Mushrooms: 1/4 cup, finely diced*
- *Half cup lean ground beef*
- *Chopped garlic: 2 teaspoons*
- *Paprika: 1/4 teaspoon*
- *Ground cumin: 1/4 teaspoon*

- *Six green olives, diced*
- *Ground cinnamon: 1/8 teaspoon*
- *Diced tomatoes: half cup*
- *One egg, lightly beaten*

Directions: In a skillet, over a medium flame, add oil, onions, and beef and cook for 3 minutes, until beef turns brown. Add mushrooms and cook for six minutes until it starts to brown. Then add paprika, cinnamon, olives, cumin, and garlic and cook for 3 minutes or more.

Add in the chopped tomatoes, and cook for a minute. Turn off the heat; let it cool for five minutes.

Lay gyoza wrappers on a flat surface add one and a half tbsp. of beef filling in each wrapper. Brush edges with water or egg, fold wrappers, pinch edges.

Put four empanadas in an even layer in an air fryer basket, and cook for 7 minutes at 400°F until nicely browned.

Serve with sauce and salad greens.

Nutrition: Calories: 342.5, Protein: 18.5g, Carbs: 12.1g, Fat: 18.6g

Air Fried Steak with Asparagus

Preparation Time: 20 minutes
Cooking Time: 30 minutes
Servings: 2

Ingredients:

- *Olive oil spray*
- *Flank steak (2 pounds)- cut into 6 pieces*
- *Kosher salt and black pepper*
- *Two cloves of minced garlic*
- *Asparagus: 4 cups*
- *Tamari sauce: half cup*
- *Three bell peppers: sliced thinly*
- *Beef broth: 1/3 cup*
- *1 Tbsp. of unsalted butter*
- *Balsamic vinegar: 1/4 cup*

Directions: Sprinkle salt and pepper on steak and rub.

In a ziploc bag, add Tamari sauce and garlic, then add steak, toss well and seal the bag.

Let it marinate for one hour to overnight.

Place asparagus and bell peppers in the center of the steak.

Roll the steak around the vegetables and close it well with toothpicks.

Preheat the air fryer. Spray the steak with olive oil spray. And place steaks in the air fryer. Cook for 15 minutes at 400°F.

Remove the steak from the air fryer and let it rest for five minute before slicing.

In the meantime, add balsamic vinegar, butter, and broth over medium flame. Mix well and reduce it by half. Add salt and pepper to taste. Pour over steaks right before serving.

Nutrition: Calories: 469.5, Protein: 29.6g, Carbs: 19.5g, Fat: 14.6g

Greek Lamb Pita Pockets

Preparation Time: 15 minutes
Cooking Time: 7 minutes
Servings: 4

Ingredients:
Dressing:

- *1 cup plain Greek yogurt*
- *1 tbsp. lemon juice*
- *1 tsp. dried dill weed, crushed*
- *1 tsp. ground oregano*
- *½ tsp. salt*

Meatballs:

- *½ lb. (227 g.) ground lamb*
- *1 tbsp. diced onion*
- *1 tsp. dried parsley*
- *1 tsp. dried dill weed, crushed*
- *¼ tsp. oregano*
- *¼ tsp. coriander*
- *¼ tsp. ground cumin*
- *¼ tsp. salt*
- *4 pita halves*

Directions: Stir dressing ingredients together and refrigerate while preparing lamb.
Combine all meatball ingredients in a bowl and stir to distribute seasonings.
Shape the meat mixture into 12 small meatballs, rounded or slightly flattened if you prefer.
Air fry at 390ºF for 7 minutes, until well done. Remove and drain on paper towels.

Nutrition: Calories: 269.5, Fat: 13.6g, Protein: 18.6g, Carbs: 17.5g, Fiber: 2g, Sugar: 1.5g

Air Fried Beef Schnitzel

Preparation Time: 10 minutes
Cooking Time: 15 minutes
Servings: 1

Ingredients:

- *One lean beef schnitzel*
- *Olive oil: 2 tablespoons*

- *Breadcrumbs: ¼ cup*
- *One egg*
- *One lemon, to serve*

Directions: Let the air fryer heat to 356F.

In a big bowl, add oil and breadcrumbs, mix well until forms a crumbly mixture. Soak beef steak in the beaten egg and dip in the breadcrumbs mixture. Place the breaded beef in the air fryer and cook at 356°F for 15 minutes.

Remove from the air fryer and serve with green salad and a slice of lemon.

Nutrition: Calories: 339.6, Protein: 19.6g, Carbs: 13.5g, Fat: 9.5g

Beef Steak Kabobs with Vegetables

Preparation Time: 5 minutes
Cooking Time: 10 minutes
Servings: 4

Ingredients:

- *Light Soy sauce: 2 tbsp.*
- *Lean beef chuck ribs: 4 cups, cut into one-inch pieces*
- *Low-fat sour cream: 1/3 cup*
- *Half onion*
- *8 skewers: 6 inch*
- *One bell peppers*

Directions: In a mixing bowl, add sour cream and soy sauce. Mix well. Add the lean beef chunks, coat well, and let it marinate for half an hour.

Cut onion, bell pepper into one-inch pieces. In water, soak skewers for ten minutes.

Add bell peppers, onions, and beef on skewers.

Let it cook for 10 minutes in a preheated air fryer at 400°F, flip halfway through. Serve with yogurt dipping sauce.

Nutrition: Calories: 267.6, Protein: 19.6g, Carbs: 14.6g, Fat: 9.3g

Beef and Ale Casserole

Preparation Time: 10 minutes
Cooking Time: 1 hour
Servings: 4

Ingredients:

- *Three tablespoons plain flour*
- *1 ½ lbs. of leg of beef or diced braising steak*
- *Three tablespoons of olive oil*
- *Two medium onions, cut into big wedges*

- *13 oz of carrots, cut into big chunks*
- *7 oz parsnip, cut into large chunks*
- *2 cups of strong ale*
- *Three tablespoons fresh thyme*
- *One bay leaf*

Directions: Heat the oven to 340 ° F.

Spread the flour on a dinner plate. Add beef in the flour.

Pour two tsp of oil into a big frying pan. Fry beef on medium heat for 2-3 minutes. Fry until each side is brown all over. Shift the meat onto a plate and set aside.

Continue following the above instructions with the remaining meat. You can add more oil if required.

Put the remaining oil in a frying pan. Heat it moderately and sauté the onions, carrots, and parsnips for five minutes.

Then put the beef and vegetables into an ovenproof casserole dish. Pour in the ale, sprinkle the thyme and bay leaf. Cover with a lid. Cook in the oven for an hour. Wait till it is properly cooked. Serve immediately.

Nutrition: Calories: 603.6, Protein: 59.3 g, Carbs: 33g, Fat: 22.1g

Rosemary Lamb Chops

Preparation Time: 30 minutes
Cooking Time: 20 minutes
Servings: 2-3

Ingredients:

- *2 tsp. oil*
- *½ tsp. ground rosemary*
- *½ tsp. lemon juice*
- *1 lb. (454 g.) lamb chops,*
- *1-inch thick*
- *Salt and pepper to taste*
- *Cooking spray*

Directions: Mix the oil, rosemary, and lemon juice and rub them into all sides of the lamb chops. Season to taste with salt and pepper.

Cover lamb chops and allow them to rest in the fridge for 15 to 20 minutes.

Spray air fryer basket with cooking spray and place lamb chops in it.

Air fry at 360ºF for 20 minutes.

Nutrition: Calories: 236.5, Fat: 12.7g, Protein: 30.6g, Carbs: 0g, Fiber: 0g

Meatloaf

Preparation Time: 10 minutes
Cooking Time: 45 minutes
Servings: 8

Ingredients

- *4 cups ground lean beef*
- *1 cup breadcrumbs, soft and fresh*
- *1/2 cup mushrooms, chopped*
- *3 garlic cloves, minced*
- *1/2 cup carrots, shredded*
- *1/4 cup beef broth*
- *1/2 cup onions, chopped*
- *2 eggs beaten*
- *3 tbsp. ketchup*
- *1 tbsp. Worcestershire sauce*
- *1 tbsp. Dijon mustard*

For the glaze

- *1/4 cup honey*
- *1/2 cup ketchup*
- *2 tsp. Dijon mustard*

Directions: In a big bowl, add the beef broth and breadcrumbs; stir well. Set it aside in a food processor, add garlic, onions, mushrooms, and carrots, and pulse on HIGH until finely chopped.

Add soaked breadcrumbs, Dijon mustard, Worcestershire sauce, eggs, lean ground beef, ketchup, and salt in a separate bowl. With your hands, combine well and make it into a loaf. Let the air fryer preheat to 390ºF. Put the meatloaf in the oven and let it cook for 45 minutes.

In the meantime, add Dijon mustard, ketchup, and brown sugar to a bowl and mix. Glaze this mix over the meatloaf when 5 minutes are left. Let it cool for 10 minutes before serving.

Nutrition: Calories: 329.6, Protein: 19.3g, Carbs: 16.3g, Fat: 9.5g

Empanadas

Preparation Time: 10 minutes
Cooking Time: 20 minutes
Servings: 2

Ingredients:

- *8 square Gyoza wrappers*
- *1 tbsp. olive oil*
- *1/4 cup white onion, finely diced*
- *1/4 cup mushrooms, finely diced*

- *1/2 cup lean ground beef*
- *2 tsp. garlic, chopped*
- *1/4 tsp. paprika*
- *1/4 tsp. ground cumin*
- *6 green olives, diced*
- *1/8 tsp. ground cinnamon*
- *1/2 cup tomatoes, diced*
- *1 egg, lightly beaten*

Directions: Add oil, onions, and beef over a medium flame in a skillet and cook for 3 minutes until the meat turns brown.

Add the mushrooms and cook for 6 minutes until it starts to brown. Then add the paprika, cinnamon, olives, cumin, and garlic and cook for 3 minutes or more.

Add in the chopped tomatoes, and cook for 1 minute; turn off the heat and let it cool for 5 minutes.

Lay the wrappers on a flat surface add 1 1/2 tbsp. of beef filling in each wrapper. Brush edges with water or egg, fold the wrappers, and pinch the edges. Put 4 empanadas in an even layer in an air fryer basket, and cook for 7 minutes at 400°F until nicely browned. Serve with sauce and salad greens.

Nutrition: Calories: 342.5, Fat: 18.5g, Protein: 18.6g, Carbs: 12.1g

Air Fryer Hamburgers

Preparation Time: 5 minutes
Cooking Time: 13 minutes
Servings: 4

Ingredients:

- *Buns:4*
- *Lean ground beef chuck: 4 cups*
- *Salt to taste*
- *Slices of any cheese: 4 slices*
- *Black Pepper, to taste*

Directions: Let the air fryer preheat to 350 F.

In a bowl, add lean ground beef, pepper, and salt. Mix well and form patties.

Put the patties in the air fryer in one layer only, cook for 6 minutes, flip them halfway through. One minute before you take out the patties, add cheese on top. When cheese is melted, take out from the air fryer.

Add ketchup, any dressing, tomatoes, lettuce and patties to your buns. Serve hot.

Nutrition: Calories: 519.6, Protein: 31.3g, Carbs: 21.6g, Fat: 33.8g

Air Fryer Meatloaf

Preparation Time: 10 minutes
Cooking Time: 45 minutes
Servings: 8

Ingredients:

- *Ground lean beef: 4 cups*
- *Bread crumbs: 1 cup (soft and fresh)*
- *Chopped mushrooms: ½ cup*
- *Cloves of minced garlic*
- *Shredded carrots: ½ cup*
- *Beef broth: ¼ cup*
- *Chopped onions: ½ cup*
- *Two eggs beaten*
- *Ketchup: 3 Tbsp.*
- *Worcestershire sauce: 1 Tbsp.*
- *Dijon mustard: 1 Tbsp.*

For Glaze:

- *Ketchup: half cup*
- *Dijon mustard: 2 tsp*

Directions: In a big bowl, add beef broth and breadcrumbs, stir well. And set it aside in a food processor, add garlic, onions, mushrooms, and carrots, and pulse on high until finely chopped.

In a separate bowl, add soaked breadcrumbs, Dijon mustard, Worcestershire sauce, eggs, lean ground beef, ketchup, and salt. With your hands, combine well and make it into a loaf. Let the air fryer preheat to 390 F.

Put Meatloaf in the Air Fryer and let it cook for 45 minutes.

In the meantime, add Dijon mustard, ketchup, and brown sugar in a bowl and mix. Glaze this mix over Meatloaf when five minutes are left. Rest the Meatloaf for ten minutes before serving.

Nutrition: Calories: 329.6, Proteins: 19.3g, Carbs: 15.4g, Fat: 9.1 g

Mini Meatloaf

Preparation Time: 15 minutes
Cooking Time: 25 minutes
Servings: 6

Ingredients

- *1 lb. 80/20 ground beef*
- *1/4 medium yellow onion, peeled and diced*
- *1/2 medium green bell pepper, seeded and diced*

- *1 large egg*
- *3 tbsp. blanched finely ground almond flour*
- *1 tbsp. Worcestershire sauce*
- *1/2 tsp. garlic powder*
- *1 tsp. parsley, dried*
- *2 tbsp. tomato paste*
- *1/4 cup water*
- *1 tbsp. powdered erythritol*

Directions: Combine the ground beef, onion, pepper, egg, and almond flour in a large bowl. Pour in the Worcestershire sauce, garlic powder and parsley to the bowl. Mix until fully combined.

Divide the mixture and place it into 2 (4-inch) loaf baking pans.

In a small bowl, mix water, tomato paste, and erythritol. Spoon half the mixture over each loaf.

Working in batches (if necessary), place loaf pans into the air fryer basket.

Set the temperature to 350°F and cook for 25 minutes.

Serve warm.

Nutrition: Calories: 169.5, Fat: 8.6g, Protein: 15.3g, Carbs: 2.5g, Fiber: 1g, Sugar: 1.8g

Hamburgers

Preparation Time: 5 minutes
Cooking Time: 6 minutes
Servings: 4

Ingredients:

- *4 buns*
- *4 cups lean ground beef chuck*
- *4 slices any cheese*
- *Black Pepper to taste*
- *2 sliced tomatoes*
- *1 head of lettuce*
- *Ketchup for dressing*
- *Salt to taste*

Directions: Let the air fryer preheat to 350ºF.

In a bowl, add ground beef, salt, and pepper. Mix well and form into patties.

Place them in the air fryer in a single layer, cook for 6 minutes, flip them halfway through.

One minute before removing the patties, add the cheese on top. When cheese is melted, remove from the air fryer.

Add ketchup, tomatoes, lettuce, and patties to your buns and serve.

Nutrition: Calories: 519.5, Carbs: 21.2g, Protein: 31.3g, Fat: 33.5g

Flavorful Meatballs

Preparation Time: 15 minutes
Cooking Time: 25 minutes
Servings: 6

Ingredients:

- *200 g ground beef*
- *200 g ground chicken*
- *100 g ground pork*
- *30 g minced garlic*
- *1 potato*
- *1 egg*
- *1 tsp. basil*
- *1 tsp. cayenne pepper*
- *1 tsp. white pepper*
- *2 tsp. olive oil*

Directions: Combine ground beef, chicken meat, and pork in the mixing bowl and stir it gently.
Sprinkle it with basil, cayenne pepper, and white pepper.
Add minced garlic and egg. Stir the mixture gently. You should get a fluffy mass.
Peel the potato and grate it. Add grated potato to the mixture and stir it again.
Preheat the air fryer oven to 375°F. Take a tray and spray it with olive oil.
Make the balls from the meat mass and put them on the tray. Lay the tray in the oven and cook it for 25 minutes.

Nutrition: Calories: 203.5, Protein: 26.5g, Fat: 7.1g, Carbs: 6.5g

Beef with Mushrooms

Preparation Time: 15 minutes
Cooking Time: 40 minutes
Servings: 4

Ingredients:

- *300 g beef*
- *150 g mushrooms*
- *1 onion*
- *1 tsp. olive oil*
- *100 g vegetable broth*
- *1 tsp. basil*
- *1 tsp. chili*
- *30 g tomato juice*

Directions: Take the beef and pierce the meat with a knife. Rub it with olive oil, basil, and chili, and lemon juice.

Chop the onion and mushrooms and pour them with vegetable broth. Cook the vegetables for 5 minutes.

Take a big tray and put the meat in it. Add vegetable broth to the tray too. It will make the meat juicy.

Preheat the air fryer oven to 375ºF and cook it for 35 minutes.

Nutrition: Calories: 174.5, Protein: 25.6g, Fat: 5.5g, Carbs: 4.1g

Taco-Stuffed Peppers

Preparation Time: 10 minutes
Cooking Time: 25 minutes
Servings: 4

Ingredients

- *1 lb. 80/20 ground beef*
- *1 tbsp. chili powder*
- *2 tsp. cumin*
- *1 tsp. garlic powder*
- *1 tsp. salt*
- *1/4 tsp. ground black pepper*
- *1 can (10 oz.) diced tomatoes and green chiles, drained*
- *4 medium green bell peppers*
- *1 cup shredded Monterey jack cheese, divided*

Directions: In a medium skillet over medium heat, brown the ground beef for about 7 minutes. When no pink remains, drain the fat from the skillet.

Return the skillet to the stovetop and add chili powder, cumin, garlic powder, salt, and black pepper. Add drained can have diced tomatoes and chiles to the skillet. Continue cooking for 3–5 minutes.

While the mixture is cooking, cut each bell pepper in half. Remove the seeds and white membrane.

Spoon the cooked mixture evenly into each bell pepper and top with a 1/4 cup of cheese. Place the stuffed peppers into the air fryer basket. Set the temperature to 350°F and cook for 15 minutes.

When done, peppers will be fork-tender, and cheese will be browned and bubbling. Serve warm.

Nutrition: Calories: 345.6, Fat: 18.5g, Protein: 28.3g, Carbs: 110.2g, Fibers: 3.2g, Sugars: 4.5g

Lamb Chops with Herb Butter

Preparation Time: 10 minutes
Cooking Time: 5 minutes
Servings: 4

Ingredients:

- *4 lamb chops*
- *1 tsp. rosemary, diced*
- *1 tbsp. butter*
- *Pepper*
- *Salt*

Directions: Season lamb chops with pepper and salt.
Place the dehydrating tray in a multi-level air fryer basket. Insert the basket in the air fryer oven.
Place the lamb chops on dehydrating tray.
Seal pot with the air fryer lid and select "Air Fry" mode, then set the temperature to 400ºF and cook for 5 minutes.
Stir in rosemary and butter and spread overcooked lamb chops. Serve and enjoy.

Nutrition: Calories: 277.5, Fat: 12.2g, Carbs: 0.2g, Sugar: 0g, Protein: 38.5g

Lemon Greek Beef and Vegetables

Preparation Time: 10 minutes
Cooking Time: 14 minutes
Servings: 4

Ingredients:

- *½ lb. (227 g.) 96% lean ground beef*
- *2 medium tomatoes, chopped*
- *1 onion, chopped*
- *2 garlic cloves, minced*
- *2 cups fresh baby spinach*
- *2 tbsp. freshly squeezed lemon juice*
- *⅓ cup low-sodium beef broth*
- *2 tbsp. crumbled low-sodium feta cheese*

Directions: In a baking pan, crumble the beef. Place in the air fryer basket. Air fry at 370ºF for 6 minutes, stirring once during cooking until browned. Drain off any fat or liquid.
Swell the tomatoes, onion, and garlic into the pan. Air fry for 4 minutes more.
Add the spinach, lemon juice, and beef broth.
Air fry for 4 minutes more, or until the spinach is wilted.
Sprinkle with the feta cheese and serve immediately.

Nutrition: Calories: 97.5, Fat: 1g, Protein: 15.5g, Carbs: 4.6g, Fiber: 1g, Sugar: 1.6g

Meatballs and Creamy Potatoes

Preparation Time: 45–50 minutes
Cooking Time: 35 minutes
Servings: 4–6

Ingredients:

- *12 oz. lean ground beef*
- *1 medium onion, finely chopped*
- *1 tbsp. parsley leaves, finely chopped*
- *½ tbsp. fresh thyme leaves*
- *½ tsp. minced garlic*
- *2 tbsp olive oil*
- *1 tsp. salt*
- *1 tsp. ground black pepper*
- *1 enormous egg*
- *3 tbsp. bread crumbs*
- *1 cup half & half, or ½ cup whole milk and ½ cup cream mixed*
- *7 medium russet potatoes*
- *½ tsp. ground nutmeg*
- *½ cup grated gruyere cheese*

Directions: Place the ground beef, onions, parsley, thyme, garlic, olive oil, salt and pepper, egg, and breadcrumbs in a bowl, and mix well. Place in refrigerator until needed.

In another bowl, place half & half and nutmeg, and whisk to combine.

Peel and wash potatoes, and then slice them thinly, ⅛ to 1/5 of an inch, if needed, to use a mandolin.

Warm up the Air Fryer to 390°F.

Place potato slices in a bowl with half & half and toss to coat well. Layer the potato slices in an Air Fryer baking accessory and pour over the leftover half & half. Bake for 25 minutes at 390°F.

Meanwhile, take the meat mixture out of the fridge and shape it into inch and half balls.

When potatoes are cooked, place meatballs on top of them in one layer and cover with the grated Gruyere.

Cook for another 10 minutes.

Nutrition: Calories: 231.2, Fat: 8g, Carbs: 5.8g, Protein: 12.8g

Pork Recipes

Paprika Pulled Pork

Preparation Time: 15 minutes
Cooking Time: 25 minutes
Servings: 4

Ingredients:

- *1 tbsp. chili flakes*
- *1 tsp. ground black pepper*
- *½ tsp. paprika*
- *1 tsp. cayenne pepper*
- *⅓ cup cream*
- *1 tsp. kosher salt*
- *1-lb. pork tenderloin*
- *1 tsp. ground thyme*
- *4 cup chicken stock*
- *1 tsp. butter*

Directions: Pour the chicken stock into the air fryer basket tray.
Add the pork steak and sprinkle the mixture with chili flakes, paprika, cayenne pepper, ground black pepper, and salt. Preheat the air fryer to 370°F and cook the meat for 20 minutes.
Strain the liquid and shred the meat with 2 forks.
Then add the butter and cream and mix it.
Cook the pulled pork for 4 minutes more at 360°F. When the pulled pork is cooked allow to rest briefly.

Nutrition: Calories: 197.5, Fat: 6.2, Fiber: 0.5g, Carbs: 2.1g, Protein: 31.2

Air Fryer Breaded Pork Chops

Preparation Time: 10 minutes
Cooking Time: 18 minutes
Servings: 4

Ingredients:

- *Whole-wheat breadcrumbs: 1 cup*
- *Salt: ¼ teaspoon*
- *Pork chops: 2-4 pieces (center cut and boneless)*
- *Chili powder: half teaspoon*
- *Parmesan cheese: 1 tablespoon*
- *Paprika: 1½ teaspoons*
- *One egg beaten*
- *Onion powder: half teaspoon*
- *Granulated garlic: half teaspoon*
- *Pepper, to taste*

Directions: Let the air fryer preheat to 400 F.

Rub salt on each side of pork chops, and let it rest.

Add beaten egg in a big bowl.

Add breadcrumbs, Parmesan cheese, paprika, garlic, pepper, chili powder, and onion powder in a bowl and mix well. Dip pork chop in beaten egg, then in breadcrumb mixture. Put it in the air fryer and spray with oil. Cook for 12 minutes at 400 F. Flip and cook for another six minutes.

Nutrition: Calories: 424.6, Protein: 31.5g, Carbs: 18.5g, Fat: 19.6g, Fiber: 5g

Air Fryer Pork Chop & Broccoli

Preparation Time: 20 minutes
Cooking Time: 10 minutes
Servings: 2

Ingredients:

- *Broccoli florets: 2 cups*
- *Bone-in pork chop: 2 pieces*
- *Paprika: half tsp.*
- *Avocado oil: 2 tbsp.*
- *Garlic powder: half tsp.*
- *Onion powder: half tsp.*
- *Two cloves of crushed garlic*
- *Salt: 1 teaspoon divided*

Directions: Let the air fryer preheat to 350F. Spray the basket with cooking oil.

Add one tbsp. Oil, garlic powder, onion powder, half tsp. of salt, and paprika in a bowl and mix well. Rub this spice mix to the pork chop's sides.

Add pork chops to air fryer basket and cook for five minutes.

In the meantime, add one tsp. oil, garlic, half tsp of salt, and broccoli to a bowl and coat well.

Flip the pork chop, add the broccoli, and cook for five more minutes.

Take out from the air fryer and serve.

Nutrition: Calories: 482.5, Protein: 23.5g, Carbs: 11.5g, Fat: 19.5g

Jamaican Pork with Jerk

Preparation Time: 10 minutes
Cooking Time: 20 minutes
Servings: 4

Ingredients:

- *Pork, cut into three-inch pieces*
- *Jerk paste: ¼ cup*

Directions: Rub jerk paste all over the pork pieces. Let it marinate for four hours in the refrigerator.

Let the air fryer preheat to 390°F. spray with olive oil.

Before putting in the air fryer, let the meat sit for 20 minutes at room temperature.

Cook for 20 minutes at 390°F in the air fryer, flip halfway through.

Take out from the air fryer and let it rest for ten minutes before slicing. Serve with microgreens.

Nutrition: Calories: 233.5, Protein: 31.5g, Carbs: 11.4g, Fat: 8.5g

Pork Tenderloin with Mustard Glazed

Preparation Time: 10 minutes
Cooking Time: 18 minutes
Servings: 4

Ingredients:

- *Yellow mustard: ¼ cup*
- *One pork tenderloin*
- *Salt: ¼ tsp*
- *Freshly ground black pepper: ⅛ tsp*
- *Minced garlic: 1 Tbsp.*
- *Dried rosemary: 1 tsp*
- *Italian seasoning: 1 tsp*

Directions: Cut the top of pork tenderloin. Add minced garlic in the cuts, and season with salt and pepper.

In a bowl, add mustard, rosemary, and Italian seasoning mix until combined. Rub this mustard mix all over pork.

Let it marinate in the refrigerator for two hours.

Put pork tenderloin in the air fryer basket. Cook for 18 minutes at 400°F. with an instant-read thermometer internal temperature of pork should be 145°F.

Take out from the air fryer and serve.

Nutrition: Calories: 389.5, Protein: 59.6g, Carbs: 10.5g, Fat: 10.4g

Cheesy Pork Chops in Air Fryer

Preparation Time: 5 minutes
Cooking Time: 8 minutes
Servings: 2

Ingredients:

- *4 lean pork chops*
- *Salt: half tsp.*

- *Garlic powder: half tsp.*
- *Shredded cheese: 4 tbsp.*
- *Chopped cilantro*

Directions: Let the air fryer preheat to 350F.

Rub the pork chops with garlic, cilantro, and salt. Put in the air fryer and let it cook for four minutes.

Flip them and cook for two minutes more.

Add cheese on top and cook for another two minutes or until the cheese is melted.

Serve with salad greens.

Nutrition: Calories: 466.5, Protein: 61.5g, Fat: 21.5g

Stuffed Cabbage and Pork Loin Rolls

Preparation Time: 5 minutes
Cooking Time: 20 minutes
Servings: 4

Ingredients:

- *500 g. white cabbage*
- *1 onion*
- *8 pork tenderloin steaks*
- *2 carrots*
- *4 tbsp. soy sauce*
- *50 g. extra virgin olive oil*
- *Salt to taste*
- *8 sheets rice*

Directions: Put the chopped cabbage in the Thermo mix glass together with the onion and the chopped carrot.

Select 5 seconds on the speed 5. Add the extra virgin olive oil. Select 5 minutes, left turn, and spoon speed.

Cut the tenderloin steaks into thin strips. Add the meat to the thermo mix glass. Select 5 minutes, room temperature, left turn, spoon speed without beaker.

Add the soy sauce. Select 5 minutes, room temperature, left turn, spoon speed. Rectify salt. Let it cold down.

Hydrate the rice slices. Extend and distribute the filling between them.

Make the rolls, folding so that the edges are completely closed. Set the rolls in the air fryer and paint with the oil.

Select 10 minutes for cooking time and set the temperature to 375°F.

Nutrition: Calories: 119.5, Fat: 3.1g, Carbs: 0g, Protein: 21.4g

12-Minute Pork Loin

Preparation Time: 10 minutes
Cooking Time: 12 minutes
Servings: 4

Ingredients:

- *One tablespoon water*
- *One tablespoon Worcestershire sauce*
- *One tablespoon lemon juice*
- *One tablespoon Dijon-style mustard*
- *Four boneless pork top loin chops*
- *Half tablespoon lemon-pepper seasoning*
- *One tablespoon butter*
- *One tablespoon snipped fresh chives*

Directions: For the sauce, combine water, Worcestershire sauce, lemon juice, and mustard in a small bowl; set aside.
Trim fat from chops. Use the lemon-pepper seasoning to sprinkle both sides of each chop. In a 10-inch pan, melt butter over medium heat. Add chops and cook for 12 minutes. Rotating once halfway through the cooking period. Withdraw from the heat. Place chops to a serving plate; protect and hold warm.
Pour the sauce into the pan; stir and extract any crusty brown pieces from the bottom of the pan. Pour the gravy over the chops. Sprinkle chives.

Nutrition: Calories: 175.4, Protein: 17.4g, Carbs: 1g, Fat: 9.8g

Pork Head Chops With Vegetables

Preparation Time: 9 minutes
Cooking Time: 24 minutes
Servings: 4

Ingredients:

- *4 pork head chops*
- *2 red tomatoes*
- *1 large green pepper*
- *4 mushrooms*
- *1 onion*
- *4 slices cheese*
- *Salt to taste*
- *Ground pepper to taste*
- *Extra-virgin olive oil*

Directions: Put the chops on a plate and season with salt and pepper.

Put 2 of the chops in the air fryer basket. Add the tomato slices, cheese slices, pepper slices, onion slices, and mushroom slices. Add some threads of oil. Cook at 375°F for 24 minutes. Check that the meat is well made and remove it.

Repeat the same operation with the other 2 pork chops.

Nutrition: Calories: 105.3, Fat: 3g, Carbs: 0g, Protein: 21.4g

Pork Trinoza Wrapped in Ham

Preparation Time: 8 minutes
Cooking Time: 9 minutes
Servings: 6

Ingredients:

- *6 pieces Serrano ham, thinly sliced*
- *454 g. pork, halved, with butter and crushed*
- *6 g. salt*
- *1 g. black pepper*
- *227 g. fresh spinach leaves, divided*
- *4 slices Mozzarella cheese, divided*
- *18 g. sun-dried tomatoes, divided*
- *10 ml olive oil, divided*

Directions: Place 3 pieces of ham on baking paper, slightly overlapping each other. Place 1 half of the pork in the ham. Repeat with the other half. Season the inside of the pork rolls with salt and pepper.

Place half of the spinach, cheese, and sun-dried tomatoes on top of the pork loin, leaving a 13 mm. border on all sides.

Roll the fillet around the filling and tie it with a kitchen cord to keep it closed.

Repeat the process for the other pork steak and place them in the fridge.

Warm in the air fryer and press START/PAUSE.

Brush the olive oil on each wrapped steak and place them in the preheated air fryer.

Select STEAK. Set the timer to 9 minutes and press START/PAUSE. Let it cool before cutting.

Nutrition: Calories: 281.5, Fat: 23g, Carbs: 0g, Protein: 16.8g

Homemade Flamingos

Preparation Time: 8 minutes
Cooking Time: 8 minutes
Servings: 4

Ingredients:

- *400 g. pork fillets, very thin sliced*
- *2 eggs, boiled and chopped*

* *100 g. Serrano ham, chopped*
* *1 egg, beaten*
* *1 cup breadcrumbs*

Directions: Make a roll with the pork fillets. Introduce half-cooked egg and Serrano ham. So that the roll does not lose its shape, fasten with a string or chopsticks.
Pass the rolls through the beaten egg and then through the breadcrumbs until it forms a good layer.
Warm the air fryer for a few minutes at 375°F. Insert the rolls in the basket and set the timer for 8 minutes.

Nutrition: Calories: 481.5, Fat: 23g, Carbs: 0g, Protein: 16.8g

Air Fryer Pork Satay

Preparation Time: 15 minutes
Cooking Time: 10 minutes
Servings: 4

Ingredients:

* *1 (1 lb./454 g.) pork tenderloin, cut into 1 1/2-inch cubes*
* *1/4 cup onion, minced*
* *2 garlic cloves, minced*
* *1 jalapeño pepper, minced*
* *2 tbsp. lime juice, freshly squeezed*
* *2 tbsp. coconut milk*
* *2 tbsp. unsalted peanut butter*
* *2 tsp. curry powder*

Directions: In a medium bowl, mix the pork, lime juice, garlic, onion, jalapeño, peanut butter, coconut milk, and curry powder until well combined. Let position for 10 minutes at room temperature.
Remove the pork from the marinade but reserve the marinade.
Thread the pork onto 8 skewers. Air fry at 380ºF for 10 minutes, brushing once with the reserved marinade until the pork reaches at least 145ºF on a meat thermometer.
Discard any remaining marinade and serve immediately.

Nutrition: Calories: 194.5, Fats: 24.5g, Protein: 7.6g, Carbs: 1g, Fibers: 1g, Sugars: 2.5g

Pulled Pork

Preparation Time: 10 minutes
Cooking Time: 2 1/2 hours
Servings: 8

Ingredients:

- *2 tbsp. chili powder*
- *1 tsp. garlic powder*
- *1/2 tsp. onion powder*
- *1/2 tsp. ground black pepper*
- *1/2 tsp. cumin*
- *4 lbs. pork shoulder*

Directions: Mix the chili powder, garlic powder, onion powder, pepper, and cumin in a small bowl.

Rub the spice mixture over the pork shoulder, patting it into the skin.

Place the meat into the air fryer basket, set the temperature to 350°F and the timer for 2 1/2 hours.

Pork skin will be crispy and meat easily shredded with 2 forks when done.

Nutrition: Calories: 536.2, Fats: 34.5g, Protein: 43.5g, Carbs: 1g, Fibers: 1g

Pork Loin

Preparation Time: 10 minutes
Cooking Time: 20 minutes
Servings: 6

Ingredients:

- *1/2 lb. pork tenderloin patted dry*
- *Non-stick cooking spray*
- *2 tbsps. garlic scape pesto*
- *Salt to taste*
- *Pepper to taste*

Directions: Adjust the temperature of the air fryer to 375°F.

Rub all sides of the tenderloin with the non-stick cooking spray. Add pepper, garlic scape pesto, and salt.

Sprinkle the air fryer basket with cooking spray.

Place the tenderloin on the air fryer and cook at 400°F for 10 minutes.

Flip over to the other side and cook for another 10 minutes.

Remove from the air fryer and serve.

Nutrition: Calories: 378.7, Fat: 1.6g, Protein: 8.5g, Carbs: 0g

Spiced Pork Chops

Preparation Time: 8 minutes
Cooking Time: 10 minutes
Servings: 2

Ingredients:

- *2 pork chops, boneless*
- *15 ml. vegetable oil*
- *25 g. dark brown sugar, packaged*
- *6 g. Hungarian paprika*
- *2 g. ground mustard*
- *2 g. freshly ground black pepper*
- *3 g. onion powder*
- *3 g. garlic powder*
- *Salt and pepper to taste*

Directions: Warm the air fryer for a few minutes at 375°F.

Cover the pork chops with oil.

Put all the spices and season the pork chops abundantly, almost as if you were making them breaded.

Place the pork chops in the preheated air fryer.

Select STEAK and set the time to 10 minutes. Remove the pork chops when it has finished cooking.

Let it stand and serve.

Nutrition: Calories: 117.5, Fat: 6.2g, Carbs: 0.3g, Protein: 13.5g

Herbed Pork Ribs

Preparation Time: 6 minutes
Cooking Time: 20 minutes
Servings: 4

Ingredients:

- *500 g. pork ribs*
- *1 tbsp. provencal herbs*
- *Salt to taste*
- *Ground pepper to taste*
- *1 tsp. oil*

Directions: Set the ribs in a bowl and add some oil, Provencal herbs, salt, and ground pepper.

Stir well and leave in the fridge for 1 hour.

Put the ribs in the basket of the air fryer and select 380°F for 20 minutes.

From time to time, shake the basket and remove the ribs.

Nutrition: Calories: 295.6, Fat: 3.1g, Carbs: 5.6g, Protein: 29.6g

Pork Ribs

Preparation Time: 5 minutes

Cooking Time: 20–25 minutes
Servings: 4

Ingredients:

- *12 pork ribs, trimmed excess fat*
- *2 tbsp. cornstarch*
- *2 tbsp. olive oil*
- *1 tsp. dry mustard*
- *½ tsp. thyme*
- *½ tsp. garlic powder*
- *1 tsp. dried marjoram*
- *Pinch salt*
- *Freshly ground black pepper, to taste*

Directions: Place the ribs on a clean work surface.
In a bowl, combine the olive oil, garlic powder, mustard, cornstarch, thyme, marjoram, salt, and pepper. Rub into the ribs.
Place the ribs in the air fryer basket and roast at 400ºF for 10 minutes.
Turn the ribs with tongs and roast for 10 minutes.

Nutrition: Calories: 578.4, Fat: 43.5g, Protein: 40.5g, Carbs: 3.7g, Fiber: 0g, Sugar: 0g

Pork Satay

Preparation Time: 15 minutes
Cooking Time: 9 minutes
Servings: 4

Ingredients:

- *1 lb. pork tenderloin, cut into 1½-inch cubes*
- *¼ cup minced onion*
- *2 garlic cloves, minced*
- *1 jalapeño pepper, minced*
- *2 tbsp. freshly squeezed lime juice*
- *2 tbsp. coconut milk*
- *2 tbsp. unsalted peanut butter*
- *2 tsp. curry powder*

Directions: In a small bowl, mix the pork, garlic, lime juice, coconut milk, jalapeño, peanut butter, onion, and curry powder until well combined.
Remove the pork from the marinade but reserve the marinade.
Thread the pork onto 8 skewers. Air fry at 380ºF for 9 minutes, brushing once with the reserved marinade.

Nutrition: Calories: 194.5, Fat: 6.7g, Protein: 25.6g, Carbs: 6.4g, Fiber: 1g, Sugar: 2.6g

Dijon Tenderloin

Preparation Time: 10 minutes
Cooking Time: 12 minutes
Servings: 4

Ingredients:

- *1 lb. pork tenderloin, cut into 1-inch slices*
- *Pinch salt*
- *Freshly ground black pepper to taste*
- *2 tbsp. Dijon mustard*
- *1 garlic clove, minced*
- *½ tsp. dried basil*
- *1 cup soft bread crumbs*
- *2 tbsp. olive oil*

Directions: Pound the pork slices and sprinkle with salt and pepper on both sides. Coat the pork with the Dijon mustard and season with basil and garlic.

On a bowl, combine the bread crumbs and olive oil. Mix well. Coat the pork slices with the bread crumb mixture.

Place the pork in the air fryer basket, leaving a little space between each piece. Air fry at 390ºF for 12 minutes or until the pork is crisp and brown.

Nutrition: Calories: 335.6, Fat: 12.6g, Protein: 33.8g, Carbs: 19.8g, Fiber: 2g, Sugar: 1.5g

Pork Burgers with Red Cabbage Slaw

Preparation Time: 20 minutes
Cooking Time: 8 minutes
Servings: 4

Ingredients:

- *½ cup Greek yogurt*
- *2 tbsp. low-sodium mustard, divided*
- *1 tbsp. freshly squeezed lemon juice*
- *¼ cup sliced red cabbage*
- *¼ cup grated carrots*
- *1 lb. lean ground pork*
- *½ tsp. paprika*
- *1 cup mixed baby lettuce greens*
- *2 tomatoes, sliced*
- *8 whole-wheat sandwich buns, cut in half*

Directions: In a small bowl, combine 1 tbsp. mustard, yogurt, cabbage, lemon juice, and carrots; mix and refrigerate.

In a medium bowl, combine the pork, paprika, and the remaining 1 tbsp. mustard. Form into 8 small patties.
Put the patties into the air fryer basket. Air fry at 400ºF for 8 minutes.
Assemble the burgers by placing a lettuce leaf on the bottom of a bun. Add a tomato slice, the patties, and the cabbage mixture. Add the top of the bun and serve.

Nutrition: Calories: 472.3, Fat: 14.5g, Protein: 35.8g, Carbs: 30.7g, Fiber: 8g, Sugar: 7.8g

Fish and Seafood

Sriracha Calamari

Preparation Time: 10 minutes
Cooking Time: 13 minutes
Servings: 2

Ingredients:

- *Club soda: 1 cup*
- *Sriracha: 1-2 Tbsp.*
- *Calamari tubes: 2 cups*
- *Flour: 1 cup*
- *Pinches of salt*
- *freshly ground black pepper*
- *red pepper flakes*

Directions: Cut the calamari tubes into rings. Submerge them with club soda. Let it rest for ten minutes.

In the meantime, in a bowl, add freshly ground black pepper, flour, red pepper, and kosher salt and mix well.

Drain the calamari and pat dry with a paper towel. Coat well the calamari in the flour mix and set aside.

Spray oil in the air fryer basket and put calamari in one single layer.

Cook at 375 ° F for 11 minutes. Toss the rings twice while cooking. Meanwhile, to make sauce, add red pepper flakes, and sriracha in a bowl, mix well.

Take calamari out from the basket, mix with sauce and cook for another two minutes more. Serve with salad green.

Nutrition: Calories: 251.5, Protein: 41.5g, Carbs: 2.8g, Fat: 38.5g

Roasted Salmon with Fennel Salad

Preparation Time: 15 minutes
Cooking Time: 10 minutes
Servings: 4

Ingredients:

- *Skinless and center-cut: 4 salmon fillets*
- *Lemon juice: 1 teaspoon (fresh)*
- *Parsley: 2 teaspoons (chopped)*
- *Salt: 1 teaspoon, divided*
- *Olive oil: 2 tablespoons*
- *Chopped thyme: 1 teaspoon*
- *Fennel heads: 4 cups (thinly sliced)*
- *One clove of minced garlic*
- *Fresh dill: 2 tablespoons, chopped*
- *Greek yogurt: 2/3 cup (reduced-fat)*

Directions: In a bowl, add half teaspoon of salt, parsley, and thyme, mix well. Rub oil over salmon, and sprinkle with thyme mixture.

Put salmon fillets in the air fryer basket, cook for ten minutes at 350°F.

In the meantime, mix garlic, fennel, yogurt, half tsp. of salt, dill, lemon juice in a bowl. Serve with fennel salad.

Nutrition: Calories: 363.5, Protein: 38.5g, Carbs: 8.5g, Fat: 29.5g

Lime-Garlic Shrimp Kebabs

Preparation Time: 5 minutes
Cooking Time: 8 minutes
Servings: 2

Ingredients:

- *One lime*
- *Raw shrimp: 1 cup*
- *Salt: 1/8 teaspoon*
- *1 clove of garlic*
- *Freshly ground black pepper*

Directions: In water, let wooden skewers soak for 20 minutes.

Let the Air fryer preheat to 350°F.

In a bowl, mix shrimp, minced garlic, lime juice, kosher salt, and pepper.

Add shrimp on skewers. Place skewers in the air fryer, and cook for 8 minutes. Turn halfway over.

Nutrition: Calories: 75.4, Protein: 13.5g, Carbs: 3.5g, Fat: 8.7g

Lemon Garlic Shrimp in Air Fryer

Preparation Time: 5 minutes
Cooking Time: 8 minutes
Servings: 2

Ingredients:

- *Olive oil: 1 Tbsp.*
- *Small shrimp: 4 cups, peeled, tails removed*
- *One lemon juice and zest*
- *Parsley: 1/4 cup sliced*
- *Red pepper flakes (crushed): 1 pinch*
- *Four cloves of grated garlic*
- *Sea salt: 1/4 teaspoon*

Directions: Let the air fryer preheat to 400°F.

Mix olive oil, lemon zest, red pepper flakes, shrimp, kosher salt, and garlic in a bowl and coat the shrimp well.

Place shrimps in the air fryer basket, coat with oil spray.

Cook at 400 F for 8 minutes. Toss the shrimp halfway through Serve with lemon slices and parsley.

Nutrition: Calories: 139.5, Protein: 20.5g, Carbs: 7.5g, Fat: 17.5g

Shrimp Rolls in Air Fryer

Preparation Time: 10 minutes
Cooking Time: 10 minutes
Servings: 4

Ingredients:

- *Deveined raw shrimp: half cup chopped (peeled)*
- *Olive oil: 2 and 1/2 tbsp.*
- *Matchstick carrots: 1 cup*
- *Slices of red bell pepper: 1 cup*
- *Red pepper: 1/4 teaspoon (crushed)*
- *Slices of snow peas: 3/4 cup*
- *Shredded cabbage: 2 cups*
- *Lime juice: 1 tablespoon*
- *Sweet chili sauce: half cup*
- *Fish sauce: 2 teaspoons*
- *Eight spring roll (wrappers)*

Directions: In a skillet, add one and a half tbsp. of olive, until smoking lightly. Stir in bell pepper, cabbage, carrots, and cook for two minutes. Turn off the heat, take out in a dish and cool for five minutes.

In a bowl, add shrimp, lime juice, cabbage mixture, crushed red pepper, fish sauce, and snow peas. Mix well

Lay spring roll wrappers on a plate. Add 1/4 cup of filling in the middle of each wrapper. Fold tightly with water. Brush the olive oil over folded rolls.

Put spring rolls in the air fryer basket and cook for 6 to 7 minutes at 390°F until light brown and crispy.

You may serve with sweet chili sauce.

Nutrition: Calories: 179.5, Protein: 17.5g, Carbs: 8.7g, Fat: 8.5g

Scallops with Tomato Sauce

Preparation Time: 5 minutes
Cooking Time: 10 minutes
Servings: 2

Ingredients:

- *Sea scallops eight jumbo*
- *Tomato Paste: 1 tbsp.*
- *Chopped fresh basil one tablespoon*
- *3/4 cup of low-fat Whipping Cream*
- *Kosher salt half teaspoon*
- *Ground Freshly black pepper half teaspoon*
- *Minced garlic 1 teaspoon*
- *Frozen Spinach, thawed half cup*
- *Oil Spray*

Directions: Take a seven-inch pan (heatproof) and add spinach in a single layer at the bottom

Rub olive oil on both sides of scallops, season with kosher salt and pepper.

On top of the spinach, place the seasoned scallops

Put the pan in the air fryer and cook for ten minutes at 350°F, until scallops are cooked completely, and internal temperature reaches 135°F. Serve immediately.

Nutrition: Calories: 258.5, Protein: 18.5g, Carbs: 5.4g, Fat: 12.5g

Fish Finger Sandwich

Preparation Time: 10 minutes
Cooking Time: 15 minutes
Servings: 3

Ingredients:

- *Greek yogurt: 1 tbsp.*
- *Cod fillets: 4, without skin*
- *Flour: 2 tbsp.*
- *Whole-wheat breadcrumbs: 5 tbsp.*
- *Kosher salt and pepper to taste*
- *Capers: 10–12*
- *Frozen peas: 3/4 cup*
- *Lemon juice*

Directions: Let the air fryer preheat.

Sprinkle kosher salt and pepper on the cod fillets, and coat in flour, then in breadcrumbs. Spray the fryer basket with oil. Put the cod fillets in the basket. Cook for 15 minutes at 400° F.

Meanwhile, cook the peas in boiling water for a few minutes. Take out from the water and blend with Greek yogurt, lemon juice, and capers until well combined.

On a bun, add cooked fish with pea puree. Add lettuce and tomato.

Nutrition: Calories: 239.5, Protein: 20.5g, Carbs: 6.5g, Fat: 11.5g

Air Fryer Sushi Roll

Preparation Time: 1 hour 30 minutes
Cooking Time: 10 minutes
Servings: 3

Ingredients:
For the Kale Salad:

- *Rice vinegar: half teaspoon*
- *Chopped kale: one and a 1/2 cups*
- *Garlic powder:1/8 teaspoon*
- *Sesame seeds: 1 tablespoon*
- *Toasted sesame oil: 3/4 teaspoon*
- *Ground ginger: 1/4 teaspoon*
- *Soy sauce: 3/4 teaspoon*

For the Sushi Rolls:

- *Half avocado - sliced*
- *Cooked Sushi Rice - cooled*
- *Whole wheat breadcrumbs: half cup*
- *Sushi: 3 sheets*

Directions:
Kale Salad: In a bowl, add vinegar, garlic powder, kale, soy sauce, sesame oil, and ground ginger. With your hands, mix with sesame seeds and set it aside.
Sushi Rolls: Lay a sheet of sushi on a flat surface. With damp fingertips, add a tablespoon of rice, and spread it on the sheet. Cover the sheet with rice, leaving a half-inch space at one end.
Add kale salad with avocado slices. Roll up the sushi, use water if needed.
Add the breadcrumbs in a bowl. Coat the sushi roll with Sriracha Mayo, then in breadcrumbs.
Add the rolls to the air fryer. Cook for ten minutes at 390 F, shake the basket halfway through.
Take out from the fryer, and let them cool, then cut with a sharp knife. Serve with light soy sauce.

Nutrition: Calories: 368.7, Protein: 26.8g, Carbs: 14.5g, Fat: 13.1g

Air Fryer Tasty Egg Rolls

Preparation Time: 10 minutes
Cooking Time: 15 minutes
Servings: 3

Ingredients:

- *Coleslaw mix: half bag*
- *Half onion*
- *Salt: 1/2 teaspoon*
- *Half cups of mushrooms*
- *Lean ground pork: 2 cups*
- *One stalk of celery*
- *Wrappers (egg roll)*

Directions: Put a skillet over medium flame, add onion and lean ground pork and cook for 5 minutes.

Add mushrooms, coleslaw mixture, salt, and celery to skillet and cook for five minutes.

Roll out the egg roll and add filling (1/3 cup), roll it up, and seal with water. Spray the rolls with oil.

Put in the air fryer for 8 minutes at 400°F, flipping once halfway through. Serve hot.

Nutrition: Calories: 244.5, Protein: 11.4g, Carbs: 8.7g, Fat: 9.8g

Air Fryer Tuna Patties

Preparation Time: 15 minutes
Cooking Time: 10 minutes
Servings: 10

Ingredients:

- *Whole wheat breadcrumbs: half cup*
- *Fresh tuna: 4 cups, diced*
- *Lemon zest*
- *Lemon juice: 1 Tablespoon*
- *1 egg*
- *Grated parmesan cheese: 3 Tablespoons*
- *One chopped stalk celery*
- *Garlic powder: half teaspoon*
- *Dried herbs: half teaspoon*
- *Minced onion: 3 Tablespoons*
- *Salt to taste*
- *Freshly ground black pepper*

Directions: In a bowl, add lemon zest, bread crumbs, salt, pepper, celery, eggs, dried herbs, lemon juice, garlic powder, parmesan cheese, and onion. Mix everything. Then add in tuna gently. Shape into patties. If the mixture is too loose, cool in the refrigerator.

Add air fryer baking paper in the air fryer basket. Spray the baking paper with cooking spray.

Spray the patties with oil.

Cook for ten minutes at 360°F. turn the patties halfway over. Serve with lemon slices.

Nutrition: Calories: 213.5, Protein: 22.5g, Carbs: 5.5g, Fat: 14.5g

Air Fried Shrimp with Sweet Chili Sauce

Preparation Time: 10 minutes
Cooking Time: 8 minutes
Servings: 4

Ingredients:

- *Whole wheat bread crumbs: 3/4 cup*
- *Raw shrimp: 4 cups, deveined, peeled*
- *Flour: half cup*
- *Paprika: one tsp*
- *Chicken Seasoning, to taste*
- *2 tbsp. of one egg white*
- *Kosher salt and pepper to taste*

Sauce:

- *Sweet chili sauce: 1/4 cup*
- *Plain Greek yogurt: 1/3 cup*
- *Sriracha: 2 tbsp.*

Directions: Let the Air Fryer preheat to 400 degrees F.
Add the seasonings to shrimp and coat well.
In three separate bowls, add flour, bread crumbs, and egg whites.
First coat the shrimp in flour, dab lightly in egg whites, then in the bread crumbs.
With cooking oil, spray the shrimp. Place the shrimps in the air fryer, cook for four minutes, turn the shrimp over, and cook for another four minutes. Serve with micro green and sauce.

For the sauce: In a small bowl, mix all the ingredients.

Nutrition: Calories: 228.7, Protein: 22.5g, Carbs: 12.4g, Fat: 9.6g

Air Fryer Crab Cakes

Preparation Time: 10 minutes
Cooking Time: 10 minutes
Servings: 6

Ingredients:

- *Crab meat: 4 cups*
- *Two eggs*
- *Whole wheat bread crumbs: ¼ cup*
- *Mayonnaise: 2 tablespoons*
- *Worcestershire sauce: 1 teaspoon*
- *Old Bay seasoning: 1 and ½ teaspoon*
- *Dijon mustard: 1 teaspoon*

- *Freshly ground black pepper to taste*
- *Green onion: ¼ cup, chopped*

Directions: In a bowl, add Dijon mustard, Old Bay seasoning, eggs, Worcestershire, and mayonnaise mix it well. Then add in the chopped green onion and mix.
Fold in the crab meat to mayonnaise mix. Then add breadcrumbs, not to over mix.
Chill the mix in the refrigerator for at least 60 minutes. Then shape into patties.
Let the air-fryer preheat to 350°F. Cook for 10 minutes. Flip the patties halfway through.
Serve with lemon wedges.

Nutrition: Calories: 217.8, Protein: 16.9g, Carbs: 5.1g, Fat: 12.5g

Catfish with Green Beans, in Southern Style

Preparation Time: 10 minutes
Cooking Time: 20 minutes
Servings: 2

Ingredients:

- *Catfish fillets: 2 pieces*
- *Green beans: half cup, trimmed*
- *Freshly ground black pepper and salt, to taste divided*
- *Crushed red pepper: half tsp.*
- *Flour: 1/4 cup*
- *One egg, lightly beaten*
- *Dill pickle relish: 3/4 teaspoon*
- *Apple cider vinegar: half tsp*
- *1/3 cup whole-wheat breadcrumbs*
- *Mayonnaise: 2 tablespoons*
- *Dill*
- *Lemon wedges*

Directions: In a bowl, add green beans, spray them with cooking oil. Coat with crushed red pepper, 1/8 teaspoon of kosher salt, and half tsp. of honey and cook in the air fryer at 400°F until soft and browned, for 12 minutes. Take out from fryer and cover with aluminum foil.
In the meantime, coat catfish in flour. Then dip in egg to coat, then in breadcrumbs. Place fish in an air fryer basket and spray with cooking oil.
Cook for 8 minutes, at 400ºF, until cooked through and golden brown.
Sprinkle with pepper and salt. In the meantime, mix vinegar, dill, relish, mayonnaise, in a bowl. Serve the sauce with fish and green beans.

Nutrition: Calories: 242.5, Protein: 33.5g, Carbs: 17.5g, Fat: 17.5g

Air Fryer Salmon With Maple Soy Glaze

Preparation Time: 6 minutes
Cooking Time: 8 minutes
Servings: 4

Ingredients:

- *1 tbsp. pure maple syrup*
- *3 tbsp. gluten-free soy sauce*
- *1 tbsp. sriracha hot sauce*
- *2 garlic cloves, minced*
- *4 fillets salmon, skinless*

Directions: In a Ziploc bag, mix sriracha, maple syrup, garlic, and soy sauce with salmon. Mix well and let it marinate for at least 30 minutes.

Let the air fryer preheat to 400°F and spray the basket with oil.

Take fish out from the marinade, pat dry. Put the salmon in the air fryer, cook for 8 minutes or longer.

In the meantime, in a saucepan, add the marinade, let it simmer until reduced to half. Add the glaze over the salmon and serve.

Nutrition: Calories: 291.9, Protein: 35.8g, Fat: 10.5g, Carbs: 4.1g, Sugars: 3.1g

Air Fryer Shrimp Scampi

Preparation Time: 5 minutes
Cooking Time: 7 minutes
Servings: 2

Ingredients:

- *4 cups raw shrimp*
- *1 tbsp. lemon juice*
- *1/2 tsp. fresh basil, chopped*
- *2 tsp. red pepper flakes*
- *4 tbsp. butter*
- *1/4 cup chives, chopped*
- *1 tbsp. chicken stock*
- *1 tbsp. garlic, minced*

Directions: Let the air fryer preheat with a metal pan to 330°F.

In the hot pan, add the garlic, red pepper flakes, and half of the butter. Let it cook for 2 minutes. Add the butter, shrimp, chicken stock, minced garlic, chives, lemon juice, basil to the pan. Let it cook for 5 minutes. Bathe the shrimp in melted butter.

Take it out from the air fryer and let it rest for 1 minute. Add the fresh basil leaves and chives and serve.

Nutrition: Calories: 286.5, Fat: 5.1g, Protein: 18.5g, Carbs: 6.3g Sugar: 2.2g

Air-Fried Crumbed Fish

Preparation Time: 10 minutes
Cooking Time: 12 minutes
Servings: 2

Ingredients

- *4 fish fillets*
- *4 tbsp. olive oil*
- *1 egg beaten*
- *1/4 cup whole-wheat breadcrumbs*

Directions: Let the air fryer preheat to 375°F.

In a bowl, mix breadcrumbs with oil. Mix well.

First, coat the fish in the egg mix (egg beaten with water) than in the breadcrumb mix. Coat well.

Place in the air fryer and let it cook for 12 minutes. Serve hot with salad green and lemon.

Nutrition: Calories: 253.8, Fat: 12.2g, Protein: 15.8g, Carbs: 17.2g, Sugars: 0.3g

Parmesan Garlic Crusted Salmon

Preparation Time: 5 minutes
Cooking Time: 15 minutes
Servings: 2

Ingredients:

- *1/4 cup whole-wheat breadcrumbs*
- *4 cups salmon*
- *1 tbsp. butter, melted*
- *1/4 tsp. freshly ground black pepper*
- *1/4 cup Parmesan cheese, grated*
- *2 tsp. garlic, minced*
- *1/2 tsp. Italian seasoning*

Directions: Let the air fryer preheat to 400°F, spray the oil over the air fryer basket.

Pat the salmon dry.

In a bowl, mix Parmesan cheese, Italian seasoning, and breadcrumbs. In another pan, mix melted butter with garlic and add to the breadcrumbs mix. Mix well.

Add kosher salt and freshly ground black pepper to salmon. On top of every salmon piece, add the crust mix and press gently.

Let the air fryer preheat to 400ºF and add salmon to it. Cook until done to your liking (about 15 minutes).

Serve hot with vegetable side dishes.

Nutrition: Calories: 339.5, Fat: 18.7g, Protein: 31.5g, Carbs: 7.1g, Sugars: 0.2g

Sesame Seeds Fish Fillet

Preparation Time: 10 minutes
Cooking Time: 12-16 minutes
Servings: 2

Ingredients:

- *1 tbsp. plain flour*
- *1 egg, beaten*
- *5 frozen fish fillets*

For the coating:

- *2 tbsp. oil*
- *1/2 cup sesame seeds*
- *1/2 tsp. Rosemary herbs*
- *5–6 biscuits crumbs*
- *Kosher salt and pepper to taste*

Directions: Sauté the sesame seeds in a pan for 2 minutes, without oil. Brown them and set it aside.

On a plate, mix all coating ingredients.

Place the aluminum foil on the air fryer basket and let it preheat at 400°F.

First, coat the fish in flour. Then in egg, then in the coating mix.

Place in the air fryer. If fillets are frozen, cook for 10 minutes, then turn the fillet and cook for another 4 minutes.

If not frozen, then cook for 8 minutes and 2 minutes.

Nutrition: Calories: 249.8, Fat: 7.8g, Protein: 20.5g, Carbs: 56.8g, Sugar: 4.2g

Lemon Pepper Shrimp in Air Fryer

Preparation Time: 6 minutes
Cooking Time: 8 minutes
Servings: 2

Ingredients

- *1 1/2 cup peeled raw shrimp, deveined*
- *1/2 tbsp. olive oil*
- *1/4 tsp. garlic powder*
- *1 tsp. lemon pepper*
- *1/4 tsp. paprika*
- *1 lemon, juiced*

Directions: Let the air fryer preheat to 400ºF.

Mix lemon pepper, olive oil, paprika, garlic powder, and lemon juice in a bowl. Mix well. Add the shrimps and coat well. Add the shrimps to the air fryer, cook for 8 minutes and top with lemon slices and serve.

Nutrition: Calories: 236.5, Fat: 5.5g, Protein: 36.5g, Carbs: 2g, Sugars 0.4g

Lime Baked Salmon

Preparation Time: 22 minutes

Servings: 2

Ingredients:

- *2 (3 oz.) salmon fillets, skin removed*
- *1/4 cup jalapeños, sliced and pickled*
- *1/2 medium lime, juiced*
- *2 tbsp. cilantro, chopped*
- *1 tbsp. salted butter; melted.*
- *1/2tsp. garlic, finely minced*
- *1 tsp. chili powder*

Directions: Place the salmon fillets into a 6-inch round baking pan.
Brush each with butter and sprinkle with chili powder and garlic.
Place the jalapeño slices on top and around salmon.
Pour half of the lime juice over the salmon and cover with foil. Place pan into the air fryer basket.
Adjust the temperature to 370ºF and set the timer for 12 minutes.
When fully cooked, salmon should flake easily with a fork and reach an internal temperature of at least 145ºF.
To serve, spritz with the remaining lime juice and garnish with cilantro.

Nutrition: Calories: 166.8, Protein: 18.5g, Fiber: 7g, Fat: 8.7g, Carbs: 5.8g

Vegetables and Salads

Cheese Stuffed Mushrooms

Preparation Time: 15 minutes
Cooking Time: 7 minutes
Servings: 3

Ingredients

- *9 large button mushrooms, stems removed*
- *1 tbsp. olive oil*
- *Salt and ground black pepper, to taste*
- *1/2 tsp. rosemary, dried*
- *6 tbsp. Swiss cheese, shredded*
- *6 tbsp. Romano cheese, shredded*
- *6 tbsp. cream cheese*
- *1 tsp. soy sauce*
- *1 tsp. garlic, minced*
- *3 tbsp. green onion, minced*

Directions: Brush the mushroom caps with olive oil; sprinkle with salt, pepper, and rosemary.

In a mixing bowl, thoroughly combine the remaining ingredients, mix them well, and divide the filling mixture among the mushroom caps. Cook in the preheated air fryer at 390°F for 7 minutes.

Let the mushrooms cool slightly before serving.

Nutrition: Calories: 344.5, Fat: 27.5g, Carbs: 10.6g, Protein: 14.8g, Sugars: 7.5g

Cabbage Wedges

Preparation Time: 10 minutes
Cooking Time: 24 minutes
Servings: 6

Ingredients:

- *1 small head of green cabbage*
- *6 strips of bacon, thick-cut, pastured*
- *1 teaspoon of onion powder*
- *½ teaspoon of ground black pepper*
- *1 teaspoon of garlic powder*
- *¾ teaspoon of salt*
- *1/4 teaspoon of red chili flakes*
- *1/2 teaspoon of fennel seeds*
- *3 tablespoons of olive oil*

Directions: Switch on the Air Fryer, insert fryer basket, grease it with olive oil, then shut with its lid, set the fryer to 350°F, and preheat for 5 minutes.

Open the fryer, add bacon strips in it, close with its lid and cook for 10 minutes until nicely golden and crispy, turning the bacon halfway through the frying.

Meanwhile, prepare the cabbage, remove the cabbage's outer leaves, and then cut it into eight wedges, keeping the core intact.

Prepare the spice mix and for this, place onion powder in a bowl, add black pepper, garlic powder, salt, red chili, and fennel and stir until mixed. Drizzle cabbage wedges with oil and then sprinkle with spice mix until well coated.

When the Air Fryer beeps, open its lid, transfer bacon strips to a cutting board and let it rest.

Add seasoned cabbage wedges into the fryer basket, close with its lid, then cook for 8 minutes at 400°F, flip the cabbage, spray with oil and continue air frying for 6 minutes until nicely golden and cooked.

When done, transfer cabbage wedges to a plate. Chop the bacon, sprinkle it over cabbage and serve.

Nutrition: Calories: 122.5, Carbs: 1.6g, Fat: 10.5g, Protein: 4.6g, Fiber: 0g, Sugar: 1g

Buffalo Cauliflower Wings

Preparation Time: 5 minutes
Cooking Time: 15 minutes
Servings: 6

Ingredients:

- *1 tablespoon of almond flour*
- *1 medium head of cauliflower*
- *1 ½ teaspoon of salt*
- *4 tablespoons of hot sauce*
- *1 tablespoon of olive oil*

Directions: Switch on the Air Fryer, insert fryer basket, grease it with olive oil, then shut with its lid, set the fryer to 400°F, and preheat for 5 minutes.

Meanwhile, cut cauliflower into bite-size florets and set aside.

Place flour in a large bowl, whisk in salt, oil, and hot sauce until combined, add cauliflower florets and toss until combined.

Open the fryer, add cauliflower florets in it in a single layer, close with its lid and cook for 15 minutes until nicely golden and crispy, shaking halfway through the frying.

When the Air Fryer beeps, open its lid, transfer cauliflower florets onto a serving plate and keep warm.

Cook the remaining cauliflower florets the same way and serve.

Nutrition: Calories: 47.5, Carbs: 0.6g, Fat: 3.5g, Protein: 1.6g, Fiber: 0.5g

Okra

Preparation Time: 10 minutes
Cooking Time: 10 minutes
Servings: 4

Ingredients:

- *1 cup of almond flour*
- *8 ounces of fresh okra*
- *1/2 teaspoon of sea salt*
- *1 cup of milk, reduced-fat*
- *1 egg, pastured*

Directions: Snap the egg in a basin, pour in the milk, and whisk until blended.
Cut the stem from each okra, then cut it into ½-inch pieces, add them into the egg and stir until well coated.
Mix flour and salt and add it into a large plastic bag.
Working on one okra piece at a time, drain the okra well by letting excess egg drip off, add it to the flour mixture, then seal the bag and shake well until okra is well coated.
Place the coated okra on a grease Air Fryer basket, coat the remaining okra pieces the same way and place them into the basket.
Switch on the Air Fryer, insert fryer basket, spray okra with oil, then shut with its lid, set the fryer to 390°F, and cook for 10 minutes, stirring okra halfway through the frying. Serve straight away.

Nutrition: Calories: 249.6, Carbs: 37.5g, Fat: 8.6g, Protein: 3.6g, Fiber: 2g

Air Fryer Vegetables & Italian Sausage

Preparation Time: 5 minutes
Cooking Time: 11 minutes
Servings: 4

Ingredients:

- *One bell pepper*
- *Italian Sausage: 4 pieces spicy or sweet*
- *One small onion*
- *1/4 cup of mushrooms*

Directions: Let the air fryer pre-heat to 400°F for three minutes.
Put Italian sausage in a single layer in the air fryer basket and let it cook for six minutes.
Slice the vegetables while the sausages are cooking.
After six minutes, reduce the temperature to 360°F. flip the sausage halfway through. Add the mushrooms, onions, and peppers in the basket around the sausage.
Cook at 360°F for 8 minutes. After a 4-minute mix around the sausage and vegetables.
Take vegetables and sausage out and serve hot with brown rice.

Nutrition: Calories: 290.5, Protein: 16.5g, Carbs: 9.8g, Fat: 20.5g

Sweet Potato Fritters

Preparation Time: 6–7 minutes
Cooking Time: 4 minutes
Servings: 4

Ingredients:

- *1 can sweet potato puree, 15 oz.*
- *½ tsp. minced garlic*
- *½ cup frozen spinach, thawed, finely chopped, and drained well*
- *1 large leek, minced*
- *1 serving flax egg*
- *¼ cup almond flour*
- *¼ tsp. sweet paprika flakes*
- *1 tsp. kosher salt*
- *½ tsp. ground white pepper*

Directions: Heat the Air Fryer to 330°F.

Place all ingredients in a bowl and mix all well. Divide into 16 balls and flatten each to the only an-inch-thick patty.

Place patties in the Air Fryer basket and cook for two minutes at 330°F. Flip and cook for 2 more minutes.

If needed, cook in batches.

Nutrition: Calories: 231.5, Fat: 7.5g, Carbs: 5.8g, Protein: 12.8g

Creamed Spinach

Preparation Time: 10 minutes
Cooking Time: 15 minutes
Servings: 2

Ingredients:

- *1/2 cup of chopped white onion*
- *10 ounces of frozen spinach, thawed*
- *1 teaspoon of salt*
- *1 teaspoon of ground black pepper*
- *2 teaspoons of minced garlic*
- *1/2 teaspoon of ground nutmeg*
- *4 ounces of cream cheese, reduced-fat, diced*
- *1/4 cup of shredded Parmesan cheese, reduced-fat*

Directions: Switch on the Air Fryer, insert fryer basket, grease it with olive oil, then shut with its lid, set the fryer at 350°F, and preheat for 5 minutes.

Meanwhile, take a 6-inches baking pan, grease it with oil, and set it aside.

Put spinach in a basin, add remaining ingredients (except for Parmesan cheese,) stir until well mixed and then add the mixture into a prepared baking pan.

Open the fryer, add pan in it, close with its lid and cook for 10 minutes until cooked and cheese has melted, stirring halfway through.

Then sprinkle Parmesan cheese on top of spinach and continue air frying for 5 minutes at 400°F. Serve straight away.

Nutrition: Calories: 272.5, Carbs: 7.5g, Fat: 22.6g, Protein: 8.6g, Fiber: 2g

Brussels sprouts

Preparation Time: 5 minutes
Cooking Time: 10 minutes
Servings: 2

Ingredients:

- *2 cups of Brussels sprouts*
- *1/4 teaspoon of sea salt*
- *1 tablespoon of olive oil*
- *1 tablespoon of apple cider vinegar*

Directions: Switch on the Air Fryer, insert fryer basket, grease it with olive oil, then shut with its lid, set the fryer to 400 ºF, and preheat for 5 minutes.

Meanwhile, cut the sprouts lengthwise into ¼-inch thick pieces, put them in a bowl, add remaining ingredients and toss until well coated.

Open the fryer, add sprouts in it, close with its lid and cook for 10 minutes until crispy and cooked, shaking halfway through the frying. When Air Fryer beeps, open its lid, transfer sprouts onto a serving plate and serve.

Nutrition: Calories: 87.5, Carbs: 10.5g, Fat: 4.1g, Protein: 4.6g, Fiber: 4g

Fried Pickles

Preparation Time: 20 minutes
Cooking Time: 10 minutes
Servings: 2

Ingredients:

- *1 egg, whisked*
- *2 tablespoons of buttermilk*
- *1/2 cup of fresh breadcrumbs*
- *1/4 cup of Romano cheese, grated*
- *1/2 teaspoon of onion powder*
- *1/2 teaspoon of garlic powder*
- *1 ½ cups of dill pickle chips, pressed dry with kitchen towels*

Mayo Sauce:

- *1/4 cup of mayonnaise*
- *1/2 tablespoon of mustard*
- *1/2 teaspoon of molasses*
- *1 tablespoon of ketchup*
- *1/4 teaspoon of ground black pepper*

Directions: In a shallow bowl, whisk the egg with buttermilk.
In another bowl, mix the onion powder, cheese, breadcrumbs, and garlic powder.
Dip the pickle chips in the egg mixture, then, dredge with the mixture.
Cook in the preheated Air Fryer at 400°F for 5 minutes; shake the basket and cook for 5 minutes more.
Meanwhile, mix all the sauce ingredients until well combined. Serve the fried pickles with the mayo sauce for dipping.

Nutrition: Calories: 341.5, Fat: 28.1g, Carbs: 12.2g, Protein: 9.8g, Sugars: 4.2g

Eggplant Parmesan

Preparation Time: 20 minutes
Cooking Time: 10 minutes
Servings: 4

Ingredients:

- *1/2 cup and 3 tablespoons almond flour, divided*
- *1.25-pound eggplant, ½-inch sliced*
- *1 tablespoon of chopped parsley*
- *1 teaspoon of Italian seasoning*
- *2 teaspoons of salt*
- *1 cup of marinara sauce*
- *1 egg, pastured*
- *1 tablespoon of water*
- *3 tablespoons of grated Parmesan cheese, reduced-fat*
- *1/4 cup of grated mozzarella cheese, reduced-fat*

Directions: Slice the eggplant into ½-inch pieces, place them in a colander, sprinkle with 1 ½ teaspoon salt on both sides, and let it rest for 15 minutes.
Meanwhile, place ½ cup flour in a bowl, add egg and water and whisk until blended.
Place remaining flour in a shallow dish, add Italian seasoning, remaining salt, and Parmesan cheese, and stir until mixed.
Switch on the Air Fryer and insert the basket. Grease with olive oil, then shut with its lid. Set the fryer to 360°F, and preheat for 5 minutes.
Meanwhile, drain the eggplant pieces, pat them dry, and then dip each slice into the egg mixture and coat with flour mixture.

Open the Air fryer, add coated eggplant slices in it in a single layer, close with its lid and cook for 8 minutes, flipping the eggplant slices halfway through the frying.

Then top each eggplant slice with a tablespoon of marinara sauce and some of the Mozzarella cheese and continue air frying for 2 minutes.

When the Air Fryer beeps, open its lid, transfer eggplants onto a serving plate, and keep them warm.

Cook the remaining eggplant slices the same way and serve.

Nutrition: Calories: 192.5, Carbs: 26.4g, Fat: 5.1g, Protein: 10.6g, Fiber: 6g

Cauliflower Rice

Preparation Time: 10 minutes
Cooking Time: 22 minutes
Servings: 3

Ingredients:
For the Tofu:

- *1 cup of diced carrot*
- *6 ounces of tofu, extra-firm, drained*
- *1/2 cup of diced white onion*
- *2 tablespoons of soy sauce*
- *1 teaspoon of turmeric*

For the Cauliflower:

- *1/2 cup of chopped broccoli*
- *3 cups of cauliflower rice*
- *1 tablespoon of minced garlic*
- *1/2 cup of frozen peas*
- *1 tablespoon of minced ginger*
- *2 tablespoons of soy sauce*
- *1 tablespoon of apple cider vinegar*
- *1 1/2 teaspoons of toasted sesame oil*

Directions: Switch on the Air Fryer, insert fryer pan, grease it with olive oil, then shut with its lid, set the fryer to 370°F, and preheat for 5 minutes.

Meanwhile, place tofu in a bowl, crumble it, then add remaining ingredients and stir until mixed.

Open the fryer, add tofu mixture in it, and spray with oil; close with its lid and cook for 10 minutes until crispy, stirring halfway through the frying.

Meanwhile, place all the ingredients for cauliflower in a bowl and toss until mixed.

When the Air Fryer beeps, open its lid, add cauliflower mixture, shake the pan to mix, and continue cooking for 12 minutes, shaking halfway through the frying. Serve straight away.

Nutrition: Calories: 257.6, Carbs: 20.1g, Fat: 12.6g, Protein: 18.8g, Fiber: 7g

Green Beans with Pecorino Romano

Preparation Time: 15 minutes
Cooking Time: 7 minutes
Servings: 3

Ingredients:

- *2 tablespoons of buttermilk*
- *1 egg*
- *4 tablespoons of cornmeal*
- *4 tablespoons of tortilla chips, crushed*
- *4 tablespoons of Pecorino Romano cheese, finely grated*
- *Coarse salt and crushed black pepper, to taste*
- *1 teaspoon of smoked paprika*
- *12 ounces of green beans, trimmed*

Directions: In a shallow bowl, whisk together the buttermilk and egg.
In a separate bowl, combine the tortilla chips, cornmeal, salt, black pepper, Pecorino Romano cheese, and paprika. Dip the green beans in the egg mixture, then, in the mixture. Place the green beans in the greased cooking basket.
Cook in the preheated Air Fryer at 390°F for 4 minutes. Shake the basket and cook for a further 3 minutes.

Nutrition: Calories: 339.5, Fat: 9.2g, Carbs: 50.1g, Protein: 13.7g, Sugars: 4.2g

Rainbow Vegetable Fritters

Preparation Time: 20 minutes
Cooking Time: 12 minutes
Servings: 2

Ingredients:

- *1 zucchini, grated and squeezed*
- *1 cup corn kernels*
- *1/2 cup canned green peas*
- *4 tablespoons all-purpose flour*
- *2 tablespoons fresh shallots, minced*
- *1 teaspoon fresh garlic, minced*
- *1 tablespoon peanut oil*
- *Sea salt and pepper, to taste*
- *1 teaspoon cayenne pepper*

Directions: In a mixing bowl, combine all ingredients until everything is well incorporated.
Shape the mixture into patties. Spritz the Air Fryer carrier with cooking spray.

Cook in the preheated Air Fryer at 365 degrees F for 6 minutes. Fit them over and cook for a further 6 minutes.

Nutrition: Calories: 214.5, Fat: 8.1g, Carbs: 31.2g, Protein: 6.5g, Sugars: 3.8g

Veggies with Yogurt-Tahini Sauce

Preparation Time: 20 minutes
Cooking Time: 16 minutes
Servings: 4

Ingredients:

- *1 pound Brussels sprouts*
- *1 pound button mushrooms*
- *2 tablespoons olive oil*
- *1/2 teaspoon white pepper*
- *1/2 teaspoon dried dill weed*
- *1/2 teaspoon cayenne pepper*
- *1/2 teaspoon celery seeds*
- *1/2 teaspoon mustard seeds*
- *Salt, to taste*

Yogurt Tahini Sauce:

- *1 cup plain yogurt*
- *2 heaping tablespoons tahini paste*
- *1 tablespoon lemon juice*
- *1 tablespoon extra-virgin olive oil*
- *1/2 teaspoon Aleppo pepper, minced*

Directions: Toss the Brussels sprouts and mushrooms with olive oil and spices. Preheat your Air Fryer to 380 degrees F. Add the Brussels sprouts to the cooking basket and cook for 10 minutes.
Add the mushrooms, turn the temperature to 390 degrees F and cook for 6 minutes more. While the vegetables are cooking, make the sauce by whisking all ingredients. Serve the warm vegetables with the sauce on the side.

Nutrition: Calories: 253.6, Fat: 16.6g, Carbs: 19.1g, Protein: 11.8g, Sugars: 7.6g

Swiss Cheese & Vegetable Casserole

Preparation Time: 50 minutes
Cooking Time: 50 minutes
Servings: 4

Ingredients:

- *1-pound potatoes, peeled and sliced (1/4-inch thick*

- *2 tablespoons olive oil*
- *1/2 teaspoon red pepper flakes, crushed*
- *1/2 teaspoon freshly ground black pepper*
- *Salt, to taste*
- *3 bell peppers, thinly sliced*
- *1 serrano pepper, thinly sliced*
- *2 medium-sized tomatoes, sliced*
- *1 leek, thinly sliced*
- *2 garlic cloves, minced*
- *1 cup Swiss cheese, shredded*

Directions: Twitch by warming your Air Fryer to 350 degrees F. Spritz a casserole dish with cooking oil.

Place the potatoes in the casserole dish in an even layer; drizzle 1 tablespoon of olive oil over the top. Then swell the black pepper, red pepper, and salt.

Add 2 bell peppers and 1/2 of the leeks. Add the tomatoes and the remaining 1 tablespoon of olive oil.

Add the leeks, remaining peppers, and minced garlic. Top with cheese.

Cover the casserole with foil and bake for 32 minutes.

Remove the foil and increase the temperature to 400 degrees F; bake for additional 18 minutes.

Nutrition: Calories: 326.5, Fat: 16.1g, Carbs: 32.6g, Protein: 13.9g, Sugars 7.1g

Roasted Broccoli with Sesame Seeds

Preparation Time: 15 minutes
Cooking Time: 10 minutes
Servings: 2

Ingredients:

- *1 pound broccoli florets*
- *2 tablespoons of sesame oil*
- *1/2 teaspoon of shallot powder*
- *1/2 teaspoon of porcini powder*
- *1 teaspoon of garlic powder*
- *Salt and pepper to taste*
- *1/2 teaspoon of cumin powder*
- *1/4 teaspoon of paprika*
- *2 tablespoons of sesame seeds*

Directions: Start by warming the Air Fryer to 400°F.

Blanch the broccoli in salted boiling water until al dente, about 4 minutes. Drain well and transfer to the lightly greased Air Fryer basket.

Add the shallot powder, porcini powder, sesame oil, cumin powder, garlic powder, salt, black pepper, paprika, and sesame seeds. Cook for 6 minutes, tossing them over halfway through the Cooking Time.

Nutrition: Calories: 266.5, Fat: 19.1g, Carbs: 19.6g, Protein: 9.6g, Sugars: 4.6g

Corn on the Cob with Herb Butter

Preparation Time: 15 minutes
Cooking Time: 8 minutes
Servings: 2

Ingredients:

- *2 ears new corn, shucked and cut into halves*
- *2 tablespoons butter, room temperature*
- *1 teaspoon granulated garlic*
- *1/2 teaspoon fresh ginger, grated*
- *Sea salt and pepper, to taste*
- *1 tablespoon fresh rosemary, chopped*
- *1 tablespoon fresh basil, chopped*
- *2 tablespoons fresh chives, roughly chopped*

Directions: Spritz the corn with cooking spray. Cook at 395 degrees F for 6 minutes, turning them over halfway through the Cooking Time.
In the time being, mix the butter with the ginger, granulated garlic, rosemary, salt, black pepper, and basil.
Spread the butter mixture all over the corn on the cob. Cook in the preheated Air Fryer an additional 2 minutes.

Nutrition: Calories 238.7, Fat: 13.1g, Carbs: 30.2g, Protein: 5.8g, Sugars 5.1g

American-Style Brussels Sprout Salad

Preparation Time: 35 minutes
Cooking Time: 15 minutes
Servings: 4

Ingredients:

- *1 pound Brussels sprouts*
- *1 apple, cored and diced*
- *1/2 cup mozzarella cheese, crumbled*
- *1/2 cup pomegranate seeds*
- *1 small-sized red onion, chopped*
- *4 eggs, hardboiled and sliced*

Dressing:

- *1/4 cup olive oil*

- *2 tablespoons champagne vinegar*
- *1 teaspoon Dijon mustard*
- *1 teaspoon honey*
- *Sea salt and ground black pepper, to taste*

Directions: Start by preheating your Air Fryer to 380 degrees F.
Add the Brussels sprouts to the cooking basket. Spritz with cooking spray and cook for 15 minutes. Let it cool to room temperature about 15 minutes.
Toss the Brussels sprouts with the apple, cheese, pomegranate seeds, and red onion.
Mix all ingredients for the dressing and toss to combine well. Serve topped with the hard-boiled eggs.

Nutrition: Calories: 318.7, Fat: 18.1g, Carbs: 26.5g, Protein: 15.2g, Sugars: 14.1g

Cauliflower Tater Tots

Preparation Time: 25 minutes
Cooking Time: 20 minutes
Servings: 4
Ingredients:

- *1 pound cauliflower florets*
- *2 eggs*
- *1 tablespoon olive oil*
- *2 tablespoons scallions, chopped*
- *1 garlic clove, minced*
- *1 cup Colby cheese, shredded*
- *1/2 cup breadcrumbs*
- *Sea salt and ground black pepper, to taste*
- *1/4 teaspoon dried dill weed*
- *1 teaspoon paprika*

Directions: Blanch the cauliflower in salted boiling water about 3 to 4 minutes until al dente. Drain well and pulse in a food processor. Add the remaining ingredients; mix to combine well. Shape the cauliflower mixture into bite-sized tots.
Spritz the Air Fryer basket with cooking spray. Cook in the preheated Air Fryer at 375 degrees F for 16 minutes, shaking halfway through the Cooking Time. Serve with your favorite sauce for dipping.

Nutrition: Calories: 266.5, Fat: 18.6g, Carbs: 9.1g, Protein: 15.4g, Sugars: 2.2g

Three-Cheese Stuffed Mushrooms

Preparation Time: 15 minutes
Cooking Time: 7 minutes

Servings: 3

Ingredients:

- *9 large button mushrooms, stems removed*
- *1 tablespoon olive oil*
- *Salt and ground black pepper, to taste*
- *1/2 teaspoon dried rosemary*
- *6 tablespoons Swiss cheese shredded*
- *6 tablespoons Romano cheese, shredded*
- *6 tablespoons cream cheese*
- *1 teaspoon soy sauce*
- *1 teaspoon garlic, minced*
- *3 tablespoons green onion, minced*

Directions: Brush the mushroom caps with olive oil; sprinkle with rosemary, salt, and pepper.
In a mixing bowl, thoroughly combine the remaining ingredients, combine it well, and divide the filling mixture among the mushroom caps. Cook in the preheated Air Fryer at 390 degrees F for 7 minutes.
Let the mushrooms cool slightly before serving.

Nutrition: Calories: 344.6, Fat: 27.6g, Carbs: 10.6g, Protein: 14.8g, Sugars: 7.6g

Side Dishes

Air Fryer Buffalo Cauliflower

Preparation Time: 5 minutes
Cooking Time: 15 minutes
Servings: 4

Ingredients:

- *Homemade buffalo sauce: 1/2 cup*
- *One head of cauliflower, cut bite-size pieces*
- *Butter melted: 1 tablespoon*
- *Olive oil*
- *Kosher salt & pepper, to taste*

Directions: Spray cooking oil on the air fryer basket.
In a bowl, add melted butter, buffalo sauce, pepper, and salt. Mix well.
Put the cauliflower bits in the air fryer and spray the olive oil over it. Let it cook at 400 F for 7 minutes.
Remove the cauliflower from the air fryer and add it to the sauce. Coat the cauliflower well. Put the sauce coated cauliflower back into the air fryer.
Cook at 400 F, for 7-8 minutes. Take out from the air fryer and serve with dipping sauce.

Nutrition: Calories: 100.8, Carbs: 3.7g, Protein: 3.5g, Fat: 6.5g

Chicken Tenders

Preparation Time: 10 minutes
Cooking Time: 15 minutes
Servings: 3

Ingredients:

- *Chicken tenderloins: 4 cups*
- *Eggs: one*
- *Superfine Almond Flour: ½ cup*
- *Powdered Parmesan cheese: ½ cup*
- *Kosher Sea salt: ½ teaspoon*
- *(1-teaspoon) freshly ground black pepper*
- *(1/2 teaspoon) Cajun seasoning*

Directions: On a small plate, pour the beaten egg.
In a bowl, mix almond flour, powered Parmesan, salt, black pepper and seasoning.
Dip each tender in egg and then in flour mixture.
Using the fork to take out the tender and place it in your air fryer basket.
Spray the air fryer and tenders with oil spray.
Cook for 12 minutes at 350°F. Raise temperature to 400°F and continue to cook for 3 minutes.

Nutrition: Calories: 279.8, Proteins: 20.6g, Carbs: 5.4g, Fat: 9.8g, Fiber 5g

Kale & Celery Crackers

Preparation Time: 10 minutes
Cooking Time: 20 minutes
Servings: 6

Ingredients:

- *One cups flax seed, ground*
- *1 cups flax seed, soaked overnight and drained*
- *2 bunches kale, chopped*
- *1 bunch basil, chopped*
- *½ bunch celery, chopped*
- *2 garlic cloves, minced*
- *1/3 cup olive oil*

Directions: Mix the ground flaxseed with the basil, kale, celery, and garlic in your food processor and mix well.
Add the oil and soaked flaxseed, then mix again.
Scatter in the pan of your air fryer, break into medium crackers and cook for 20 minutes at 380 degrees F.

Nutrition: Calories: 142.7, Fat: 1g, Fiber: 2g, Carbs: 7.8g, Protein: 4.5g

Air Fryer Spanakopita Bites

Preparation Time: 10 minutes
Cooking Time: 12 minutes
Servings: 4

Ingredients:

- *4 sheets phyllo dough*
- *Baby spinach leaves: 2 cups*
- *Grated Parmesan cheese: 2 tablespoons*
- *Low-fat cottage cheese: 1/4 cup*
- *Dried oregano: 1 teaspoon*
- *Feta cheese: 6 tbsp. crumbled*
- *Water: 2 tablespoons*
- *One egg white only*
- *Lemon zest: 1 teaspoon*
- *Cayenne pepper: 1/8 teaspoon*
- *Olive oil: 1 tablespoon*
- *Kosher salt and freshly ground black pepper: 1/4 teaspoon, each*

Directions: In a pot over high heat, add water and spinach, cook until wilted. Drain it and cool for ten minutes. Squeeze out excess moisture.

In a bowl, mix Parmesan cheese, cottage cheese, egg white, cayenne pepper, spinach, oregano, salt, black pepper, feta cheese, and zest. Mix it well.

Lay one phyllo sheet on a flat surface. Spray with oil. Add the second sheet of phyllo on top—spray oil. Add a total of 4 oiled sheets.

Form 16 strips from these four oiled sheets. Add one tbsp. of filling in one strip. Roll it around the filling.

Spray the air fryer basket with oil. Put eight bites in the basket and cook for 12 minutes at 375°F until golden brown. Flip halfway through.

Nutrition: Calories: 81.7, Fat: 3.8g, Protein: 3.6g, Carbs: 6.7g

Air Fryer Onion Rings

Preparation Time: 105 minutes
Cooking Time: 10 minutes
Servings: 4

Ingredients:

- *1 egg whisked*
- *One large onion*
- *Whole-wheat breadcrumbs: 1 and 1/2 cup*
- *Smoked paprika: 1 teaspoon*
- *Flour: 1 cup*
- *Garlic powder: 1 teaspoon*
- *Buttermilk: 1 cup*
- *Kosher salt and pepper to taste*

Directions: Cut the stems of the onion. Then cut into half-inch-thick rounds.

In a bowl, add flour, paprika, garlic powder, pepper, and salt. Then add egg and buttermilk. Mix to combine.

In another bowl, add the breadcrumbs.

Coat the onions in buttermilk mix, then in breadcrumbs mix. Freeze these breaded onions for 15 minutes.

Spray the fryer basket with oil spray.

Put onions in the air fryer basket in one single layer. Spray the onion with cooking oil.

Cook at 370 degrees F for 10-12 minutes. Flip only, if necessary.

Nutrition: Calories: 204.8, Fat: 5.1g, Carbs: 7.2g, Protein: 18.5g

Air Fryer Egg Rolls

Preparation Time: 10 minutes

Cooking Time: 20 minutes
Servings: 3

Ingredients:

- *Coleslaw mix: half bag*
- *Half onion*
- *Salt: 1/2 teaspoon*
- *Half cups of mushrooms*
- *Lean ground pork: 2 cups*
- *One stalk of celery*
- *Wrappers (egg roll)*

Directions: Put a skillet over medium flame, add onion and ground pork and cook for 5-7 minutes.
Add mushrooms, coleslaw mixture, salt, and celery to skillet and cook for 5 minutes.
Lay egg roll wrapper flat and add filling (1/3 cup), roll it up, seal with water.
Spray with oil the rolls.
Put in the air fryer for 8 minutes at 400°F, flipping once halfway through.

Nutrition: Calories: 244.8, Fat: 9.5g, Carbs: 8.5g, Protein: 11.5g

Air Fryer Chicken Nuggets

Preparation Time: 15 minutes
Cooking Time: 8 minutes
Servings: 4

Ingredients:

- *Olive oil spray*
- *Skinless boneless: 2 chicken breasts, cut into bite pieces*
- *Half tsp. of kosher salt & freshly ground black pepper to taste*
- *Grated parmesan cheese: 2 tablespoons*
- *Italian seasoned breadcrumbs: 6 tablespoons (whole wheat)*
- *Whole wheat breadcrumbs: 2 tablespoons*
- *Olive oil: 2 teaspoons*

Directions: Let the air fryer preheat for 8 minutes, to 400°F.
In a mixing bowl, add parmesan cheese, panko, and breadcrumbs and mix well.
Sprinkle kosher salt, pepper, and olive oil on chicken, and mix well.
Take a few pieces of chicken, dunk them into breadcrumbs mixture.
Cook in an Air Fryer - sprayed with olive oil - for 8 minutes, turning halfway through.

Nutrition: Calories: 187.6, Carbs: 7.8g, Protein: 25.6g, Fat: 4.1g

Zucchini Parmesan Chips

Preparation Time: 10 minutes
Cooking Time: 8 minutes
Servings: 6

Ingredients:

- *Seasoned, whole wheat Breadcrumbs: ½ cup*
- *Thinly slices of two zucchinis*
- *Parmesan Cheese: ½ cup (grated)*
- *1 Egg whisked*
- *Kosher salt and pepper, to taste*

Directions: Pat dry the zucchini slices so that no moisture remains.
In a bowl, whisk the egg with a few tsp. of water, pepper and salt.
In another bowl, mix the grated cheese and breadcrumbs.
Coat zucchini slices in egg mix then in breadcrumbs. Put all in a rack and spray with olive oil.
Add in the air fryer In a single layer, and cook for 8 minutes at 350 F.
Add salt and pepper on top if needed.

Nutrition: Calories: 100.3, Fat: 7.8g, Carbs: 5.4g, Protein: 10.8g

Zucchini Gratin

Preparation Time: 10 minutes
Cooking Time: 15 minutes
Servings: 4

Ingredient:

- *Olive oil: 1 tablespoon*
- *Chopped fresh parsley: 1 tablespoon*
- *Whole wheat bread crumbs: 2 tablespoons*
- *Medium zucchini*
- *Freshly ground black pepper & kosher salt to taste*
- *Grated Parmesan cheese: 4 tablespoons*

Directions: Let the air fryer preheat to 375°F.
Cut zucchini in half, and a further cut in eight pieces. Place in the air fryer, but do not start frying.
In a bowl, add cheese, parsley, black pepper, salt, bread crumbs, and oil. Mix well.
Add the mixture on top of the zucchini. Then cook the pieces for 15 minutes.

Nutrition: Calories: 80.9, Protein: 3.9g, Carbs: 5.8g, Fat: 4.9g

Air Fryer Zucchini Chips

Preparation Time: 10 minutes

Cooking Time: 10 minutes
Servings: 2

Ingredients:

- *Parmesan Cheese: 3 Tbsp.*
- *Garlic Powder: 1/4 tsp*
- *Zucchini: 1 Cup (thin slices)*
- *Corn Starch: 1/4 Cup*
- *Onion Powder: 1/4 tsp*
- *Salt: 1/4 tsp*
- *Whole wheat Bread Crumbs: 1/2 Cup*
- *2 beaten eggs*

Directions: Preheat the Air Fryer to 390°F.
Cut the zucchini into thin slices, like chips.
In a food processor bowl, mix garlic powder, parmesan cheese, bread crumbs, salt, and onion powder. Blend into finer pieces.
In three separate bowls, add corn starch in one, egg mix in another bowl, and breadcrumb mixture in the other bowl.
Coat zucchini chips into corn starch mix, in egg mix, then in bread crumbs.
Spray the air fryer basket with olive oil.
Add breaded zucchini chips in a single layer in the air fryer and spray with olive oil.
Air fry for ten minutes at preheated temperature.

Nutrition: Calories: 218.7, Fat: 27.1g, Carbs: 10.9g, Protein: 14.5g

Air Fryer Avocado Fries

Preparation Time: 10 minutes
Cooking Time: 10 minutes
Servings: 2

Ingredients:

- *One avocado*
- *One egg*
- *Whole wheat bread crumbs: 1/2 cup*
- *Salt: 1/2 teaspoon*

Directions: Cut the avocado into wedges.
In a bowl, beat egg with salt. In another bowl, add the bread crumbs.
Coat wedges in egg, then in crumbs.
Air fry them at 400°F for 8-10 minutes. Toss halfway through.

Nutrition: Calories: 250.5, Carbs: 18.7g, Protein: 6.5g, Fat: 16.5g

Avocado Egg Rolls

Preparation Time: 15 minutes
Cooking Time: 6 minutes
Servings: 10

Ingredients:

- *Ten egg roll wrappers*
- *Diced sundried tomatoes: ¼ cup oil drained*
- *Avocados, cut in cube*
- *Red onion: 2/3 cup chopped*
- *1/3 cup chopped cilantro*
- *Kosher salt and freshly ground black pepper*
- *Two small limes: juice*

Directions: In a bowl, add pepper, sundried tomatoes, lime juice, cilantro, avocado, onion, and salt. Then mix well.
Lay egg roll wrapper flat on a surface, add ¼ cup of filling in the wrapper's bottom.
Seal with water and make it into a roll. Spray the rolls with olive oil.
Cook at 400°F in the air fryer for six minutes. Turn halfway through.

Nutrition: Calories: 159.6, Fat: 18.7g, Carbs: 5.1g, Protein: 19.8g

Air-Fried Spinach Frittata

Preparation Time: 5 minutes
Cooking Time: 10 minutes
Servings: 4

Ingredients:

- *1/3 cup of packed spinach*
- *One small chopped red onion*
- *Shredded mozzarella cheese*
- *Three eggs*
- *Salt, pepper*
- *Olive oil*

Directions: Let the air fryer preheat to 375°F.
In a skillet over a medium flame, add oil and onion, and cook until translucent. Add spinach and sauté until half cooked.
Beat eggs and season with salt and pepper—mix spinach mixture in it.
Cook in the air fryer for 8 minutes.

Nutrition: Calories: 123.5, Fat: 11.2g, Carbs: 13.8g, Protein: 17.4g

Cheesy Bell Pepper Eggs

Preparation Time: 10 minutes
Cooking Time: 15 minutes
Servings: 4

Ingredients:

- *4 medium green bell peppers*
- *3 ounces cooked ham, chopped*
- *1/4 medium onion, peeled and chopped*
- *8 large eggs*
- *1 cup mild Cheddar cheese*

Directions: Cut each bell pepper from its tops. Pick the seeds with a small knife and the white membranes. Place onion and ham into each pepper.
Break two eggs into each chili pepper. Cover with 1/4 cup of peppered cheese. Put the basket into the air fryer.
Set the temperature to 390 ° F and change the timer for 15 minutes.
Peppers will be tender when fully fried, and the eggs will be solid. Serve hot.

Nutrition: Calories: 313.8, Protein: 25.2g, Fiber: 1.7g, Fat: 18.2g, Carbs: 5.9g

Air Fryer Egg Cups

Preparation Time: 10 minutes
Cooking Time: 10 minutes
Servings: 4

Ingredients:

- *Toasted bread: 4 slices (whole-wheat)*
- *Cooking spray, nonstick*
- *Large eggs: 4*
- *Margarine: 1 and a half tbsp. (trans-fat free)*
- *Ham: 1 slice*
- *Salt: 1/8 tsp*
- *Black pepper: 1/8 tsp*

Directions: Let the air fryer Preheat to 375°F, with the air fryer basket.
Take four ramekins, spray with cooking spray. Trim off the crusts from bread, add margarine to one side.
Put the bread down, into a ramekin, margarine-side in. Press it in the cup.
Cut the ham in strips, half-inch thick, and add on top of the bread.
Add one egg to the ramekins. Add salt and pepper.
Put the custard cups in the air fryer. Air fry at 375 F for 10 minutes.

Nutrition: Calories: 149.8, Fat: 7.8g, Carbs: 5.6g, Protein: 12.3g

Air Fryer Lemon-Garlic Tofu

Preparation Time: 20 minutes
Cooking Time: 15 minutes
Servings: 2

Ingredients:

- *Cooked quinoa 2 cups*
- *Lemons: two zest and juice*
- *Sea salt & white pepper: to taste*
- *Tofu: one block - pressed and sliced into half pieces*
- *Garlic – minced: 2 cloves*

Directions: Add the tofu into a deep dish.
In another small bowl, add the lemon zest, lemon juice, garlic, salt, and pepper.
Pour this marinade over tofu in the dish. Let it marinate for 15 minutes.
Add the tofu to the air fryer basket and air fry at 370°F for 15 minutes. Shake the basket after 8 minutes of cooking.
In a big deep bowl, add the cooked quinoa with the lemon-garlic tofu.

Nutrition: Calories: 186.8, Fat: 8.7g, Protein: 21.3g, Carbs: 7.7g

Sweet Potato Cauliflower Patties

Preparation Time: 20 minutes
Cooking Time: 20 minutes
Servings: 7

Ingredients:

- *1 green onion, chopped*
- *1 large sweet potato, peeled*
- *1 tsp. garlic, minced*
- *1 cup cilantro leaves*
- *2 cup cauliflower florets*
- *1/4 tsp. ground black pepper*
- *1/4 tsp. salt*
- *1/4 cup sunflower seeds*
- *1/4 tsp. cumin*
- *1/4 cup ground flaxseed*
- *1/2 tsp. red chili powder*
- *2 tbsp. ranch seasoning mix*
- *2 tbsp. arrowroot starch*

Directions: Cut peeled sweet potato into small pieces, then place them in a food processor and pulse until pieces are broken up.

Then add the garlic, cauliflower florets, onion, and pulse; add the remaining ingredients and pulse more until well combined.

Tip the mixture into a bowl, shape it into 7 1 1/2-inch thick patties, each about 1/4 cup, then place them on a baking sheet and freeze for 10 minutes.

Switch on the air fryer, insert the fryer basket, and grease it with olive oil; close the lid, set the fryer at 400°F, and preheat for 10 minutes.

Open the fryer, add patties to it in a single layer, and cook for 20 minutes; flipping the patties halfway through the frying.

When the air fryer beeps, open the lid, transfer the patties onto a serving plate, and keep them warm.

Prepare the continuing patties in the same way and serve.

Nutrition: Calories: 84.5, Carbs: 8.7g, Fat: 2.8g, Protein: 3.2g, Fiber: 3.5g

Crispy Brussels sprouts

Preparation Time: 5 minutes
Cooking Time: 15 minutes
Servings: 4

Ingredients:

- *Almonds sliced: 1/4 cup*
- *Brussel sprouts: 2 cups*
- *Kosher salt*
- *Parmesan cheese: 1/4 cup grated*
- *Olive oil: 2 Tablespoons*
- *Everything bagel seasoning: 2 Tablespoons*

Directions: In a saucepan, add Brussel sprouts with two cups of water and let it cook over medium flame for ten minutes. Drain the sprouts and cut in half.

In a mixing bowl, add sliced brussel sprout with parmesan cheese, crushed almonds, oil, salt, and everything bagel seasoning. Completely coat the sprouts.

Cook in the air fryer for 12-15 minutes at 375 °F.

Nutrition: Calories: 154.5, Carbs: 2.7g, Protein: 5.8g, Fat: 2.7g

Vegetable Spring Rolls

Preparation Time: 10 minutes
Cooking Time: 15 minutes
Servings: 4

Ingredients:

- *Toasted sesame seeds*

- *Large carrots – grated*
- *Spring roll wrappers*
- *One egg white*
- *Gluten-free soy sauce, a dash*
- *Half cabbage: sliced*
- *Olive oil: 2 tbsp.*

Directions: In a pan over high flame heat, 2 tbsp. of oil and sauté the chopped vegetables. Then add soy sauce.

Turn off the heat and add toasted sesame seeds.

Lay spring roll wrappers flat on a surface and add egg white with a brush on the sides.

Add some vegetable mix in the wrapper and fold.

Spray the spring rolls with oil spray and air fry for 8 minutes at 400°F. Serve with dipping sauce.

Nutrition: Calories: 128.2, Fat: 16.7g, Carbs: 7.8g, Protein: 12.4g

Asparagus Avocado Soup

Preparation Time: 10 minutes
Cooking Time: 15 minutes
Servings: 4

Ingredients:

- *1 avocado, peeled, pitted, cubed*
- *12 oz. asparagus*
- *1/2 tsp. ground black pepper*
- *1 tsp. garlic powder*
- *1 tsp. sea salt*
- *2 tbsp. olive oil, divided*
- *1/2 lemon, juiced*
- *2 cups vegetable stock*

Directions: Set the fryer to 425°F, and preheat for 5 minutes.

Meanwhile, place the asparagus in a shallow dish, sprinkle with 1 tbsp. of oil, garlic powder, salt, and black pepper, and toss until mixed.

Open the fryer, add the asparagus, and cook for 10 minutes until roasted, shaking halfway through the frying.

Transfer asparagus to a food processor. Add the remaining ingredients into a food processor and pulse until well combined and smooth.

Tip the soup in a saucepan, pour in the water if it is too thick, and heat it over medium-low heat for 5 minutes until thoroughly heated. Ladle the soup into bowls and serve.

Nutrition: Calories: 207.8, Carbs: 12.8g, Fat: 15.4g, Protein: 6.3g, Fiber: 5g

Desserts

Tahini Oatmeal Chocolate Chunk Cookies

Preparation Time: 10 minutes
Cooking Time: 5 minutes
Servings: 8

Ingredients:

- *1/3 cup of tahini*
- *1/4 cup of walnuts*
- *1/4 cup of maple syrup*
- *1/4 cup of Chocolate chunks*
- *1/4 tsp of sea salt*
- *Two tablespoons of almond flour*
- *One teaspoon of vanilla*
- *1 cup of gluten-free oat flakes*
- *One teaspoon of cinnamon*

Directions: Let the air fryer Preheat to 350 F.
In a big bowl, add cinnamon, the tahini, maple syrup, salt, and vanilla. Mix well. Then add in the walnuts, oat flakes, and almond flour. Then fold the chocolate chunks.
Take a full tablespoon of mixture, separate into eight amounts.
Line the air fryer basket with parchment paper and place cookies in one single layer.
Let them cook for 5-6 minutes at 350°F.

Nutrition: Calories: 185, Protein: 12.5g, Carbs: 17.9g, Fat: 11.4g

Grain-free Lava Cakes in Air Fryer

Preparation Time: 5 minutes
Cooking Time: 12 minutes
Servings: 2

Ingredients:

- *Two large eggs*
- *Half cup of dark chocolate chips*
- *2 tbsp. of coconut flour*
- *Two tablespoons of sugar substitute*
- *A dash of sea salt*
- *Half teaspoon of baking soda*
- *Butter and cocoa powder for two small ramekins*
- *1/4 cup of butter*

Directions: Let the air fryer preheat to 370 degrees F.

Grease the ramekins with soft butter and sprinkle with cocoa powder. It will stick to the butter. Turn the ramekins upside down, so excess cocoa powder will fall out. Set it aside.

In a microwave, safe bowl, melt the butter and chocolate chips together, stir every 15 seconds. Make sure to mix well to combine.

In a large bowl, crack the eggs and whisk with sugar substitute, mix well. Add in the salt, baking soda, and coconut flour. Fold everything.

Add the melted chocolate chip and butter mixture. Mix well, so everything combines. Pour the batter in those two prepared ramekins.

Let them air fry for ten minutes. Then take them out from the air fryer and let it cool for 3-4 minutes.

Nutrition: Calories: 215.8, Protein: 10.2g, Carbs: 13.5g, Fat: 12.2g

Raspberry Cookies in Air Fryer

Preparation Time: 15 minutes
Cooking Time: 7 minutes
Servings: 10

Ingredients:

- *One teaspoon of baking powder*
- *One cup of almond flour*
- *Three tablespoons of natural low-calorie sweetener*
- *One large egg*
- *Three and a half tablespoons raspberry (reduced-sugar) preserves*
- *Four tablespoons of softened cream cheese*

Directions: In a large bowl, add egg, flour, sweetener, baking powder, and cream cheese, mix well until a dough wet forms. Chill the dough in the fridge for 20 minutes.

Let the air fryer preheat to 400°F, add the parchment paper to the air fryer basket.

Make ten balls from the dough and put them in the prepared air fryer basket.

With your clean hands, make an indentation from your thumb in the center of every cookie.

Add one teaspoon of the raspberry preserve in the thumb hole.

Bake in the air fryer for seven minutes.

Let the cookies cool completely in the parchment paper for almost 15 minutes.

Nutrition: Calories: 110.2, Protein: 3.8g, Carbs: 8.3g, Fat: 8.8g

Sugar-Free Carrot Cake

Preparation Time: 15 minutes
Cooking Time: 30 minutes
Servings: 8

Ingredients:

- *All-Purpose Flour: 1 ¼ cups*

- *Pumpkin Pie Spice: 1 tsp*
- *Baking Powder: one teaspoon*
- *Splenda: 3/4 cup*
- *Carrots: 2 cups–grated*
- *2 Eggs*
- *Baking Soda: half teaspoon*
- *Canola Oil: ¾ cup*

Directions: Let the air fryer preheat to 350 F.

Spray the cake pan with oil spray, and add a pinch of flour over that. In a bowl, combine the flour, baking powder, pumpkin pie spice, and baking soda.

In another bowl, mix oil, the eggs, and Splenda. Now combine the dry to wet ingredients. Add in the grated carrots.

Add the cake batter to the greased cake pan. Place in the basket of the air fryer. Let it Air fry for half an hour.

Nutrition: Calories: 285.8, Fat: 20.8g, Carbs: 17.8g, Protein: 4.3g

Low Carb Peanut Butter Cookies

Preparation Time: 20 minutes
Cooking Time: 40 minutes
Servings: 24 cookies

Ingredients:

- *All-natural 100% peanut butter: 1 cup*
- *One whisked egg*
- *Liquid stevia drops: 1 teaspoon*
- *Sugar alternative: 1 cup*

Directions: Mix all the ingredients into a dough and make 24 balls.

On a cutting board, press the dough balls with the help of a fork to form a crisscross pattern.

Add six cookies to the basket of air fryer in a single layer. Make sure the cookies are separated from each other. Cook in batches.

Let them Air Fry, for 8-10 minutes, at 325°F.

Take the basket out from the air fryer and let the cookies cool for one minute, then with care, take the cookies out.

Keep baking the rest of the cookies in batches. Let them cool completely and serve.

Nutrition: Calories: 197.8, Protein: 9.8g, Carbs: 5.9g, Fat: 15.8g

Banana Muffins in Air Fryer

Preparation Time: 10 minutes

Cooking Time: 30 minutes
Servings: 8

Ingredients:
Wet Mix:

- *3 tbsp. of milk*
- *Four Cavendish size, ripe bananas*
- *Half cup sugar alternative*
- *One teaspoon of vanilla essence*
- *Two large eggs*

Dry Mix:

- *One teaspoon of baking powder*
- *One and a 1/4 cup of whole wheat flour*
- *One teaspoon of baking soda*
- *One teaspoon of cinnamon*
- *2 tbsp. of cocoa powder*
- *One teaspoon of salt*

Directions: With the fork, in a bowl, mash up the bananas, add all the wet ingredients to it, and mix well.
Sift all the dry ingredients so they combine well. Add into the wet ingredients. Carefully fold both ingredients together. Then add in the chopped walnuts, and slices of dried up fruits.
Let the air fryer preheat to 260°F.
Spray muffin cups with oil, and add the batter into. Air fryer for at least half an hour.
Take out from the air fryer and let them cool down before serving.

Nutrition: Calories: 210.8, Protein: 12.5g, Carbs: 17.5g, Fat: 11.5g

Eggless Cake

Preparation Time: 5 minutes
Cooking Time: 10 minutes
Servings: 8

Ingredients:

- *Olive Oil: 2 Tbsp.*
- *All-Purpose Flour: 1/4 Cup*
- *Cocoa Powder: 2 Tbsp.*
- *Baking Soda: 1/8 Tsp*
- *Sugar substitute: 3 Tbsp.*
- *One tablespoon of Warm Water*
- *Milk: 3 Tbsp.*
- *Two Drops of Vanilla Extract*
- *4 Raw Almonds for decoration – roughly chopped*

- *A Pinch of Salt*

Directions: Let the air fryer preheat to 370°F for two minutes.
In a large bowl, add sugar substitute, some water, milk, and oil. Whisk until a smooth batter forms.
Then add salt, cocoa powder, all-purpose flour, and baking soda, sift them into wet ingredients, and mix to form a paste.
Spray a four-inch baking pan with oil and pour the batter into it. Then add in the chopped up almonds on top of it.
Put the baking pan in the preheated air fryer. And cook for ten minutes.
Take out from the air fryer and let it cool completely before slicing.

Nutrition: Calories: 120.5, Protein: 2.2g, Carbs: 18.2g, Fat: 7.3g

Air Fried Chocolate Soufflé

Preparation Time: 15 minutes   **Cooking Time: 15 minutes**
Servings: 2

Ingredients:

- *Milk: 1/3 cup*
- *Butter soft to melted: 2 tbsp.*
- *Flour: 1 tbsp.*
- *Splenda: 2 tbsp.*
- *One Egg Yolk*
- *Sugar-Free Chocolate Chips: 1/4 cup*
- *Two egg whites*
- *Half teaspoon of cream of tartare*
- *Half teaspoon of Vanilla Extract*

Directions: Grease the ramekins with softened butter. Sprinkle with Splenda, make sure to cover them.
Let the air fryer preheat to 325-330 F.
Melt the chocolate in a microwave-safe bowl. Mix every 30 seconds until fully melted.
Melt the one and a half tablespoons of butter over low-medium heat, in a small-sized skillet.
Once the butter has melted, then whisk in the flour. Keep whisking until thickened. Then turn the heat off.
Add the egg whites with cream of tartar, with the whisk attachment, in a stand mixer, mix until peaks forms.
Meanwhile, combine the ingredients in a melted chocolate bowl, add the flour mixture and melted butter to chocolate, and blend. Add in the egg yolks, vanilla extract, remaining Splenda.
Fold the egg white peaks with the ingredients into the bowl.
Add the mix into ramekins about 3/4 full of five-ounce ramekins.
Let it bake for 12-14 minutes.

Nutrition: Calories: 287.2, Protein: 6.2g, Carbs: 4.7g, Fat: 23.9g

Berry Cheesecake

Preparation Time: 10 minutes
Cooking Time: 50 minutes
Servings: 8

Ingredients:

- *Half cup raspberries*
- *Two blocks of softened cream cheese, 8 ounce*
- *Vanilla extract: 1 teaspoon*
- *1/4 cup of strawberries*
- *Two eggs*
- *1/4 cup of blackberries*
- *One cup and 2 tbsp. of sweetener*

Directions: In a big mixing bowl, whip the sweetener and cream cheese, mix with a whip until smooth and creamy. Then add vanilla extract and eggs, again mix well.
In a food processor, pulse the berries and fold into the cream cheese, mix with two extra tbsp. of sweetener.
Take a springform pan and spray the oil, pour in the mixture.
Put the pan in the air fryer, and let it cook for 50 minutes at 300°F.
Take out from the air fryer and cool a bit before chilling in the fridge. Keep in the fridge for 2-4 hours.

Nutrition: Calories: 223.8, Protein: 12.5g, Carbs: 16.5g, Fat: 15.4g

Air Fryer Brownies

Preparation Time: 10 minutes
Cooking Time: 10 minutes
Servings: 2

Ingredients:

- *2 tbsp. of Baking Chips*
- *1/3 cup of Almond Flour*
- *One Egg*
- *Half teaspoon of Baking Powder*
- *3 tbsp. of Powdered Sweetener*
- *2 tbsp. of Cocoa Powder (Unsweetened)*
- *2 tbsp. of chopped Pecans*
- *4 tbsp. of melted Butter*

Directions: Let the air fryer preheat to 350°F.

In a large bowl, add cocoa powder, powdered sweetener, almond flour, and baking powder, give it a good mix.

Add melted butter and crack in the egg in the dry ingredients. Mix well until combined and smooth.

Fold in the chopped pecans and baking chips.

Take two ramekins to grease them well with softened butter. Add the melted batter.

Bake for ten minutes in the Air Fryer, making sure to place them as far from the heat source from the top.

Take the brownies out from the air fryer and let them cool for five minutes.

Nutrition: Calories: 200.8, Protein: 8.3g, Carbs: 12,.8g, Fat: 9.8g

Air Fryer Apple Fritter

Preparation Time: 10 minutes
Cooking Time: 14 minutes
Servings: 3

Ingredients:

- *Half apple peeled, finely chopped*
- *Half cup of All-Purpose Flour*
- *One teaspoon of Baking Powder*
- *1/4 teaspoon of Kosher Salt*
- *Half teaspoon of Ground Cinnamon*
- *2 Tbsp. of sugar alternative*
- *1/8 teaspoon of Ground Nutmeg*
- *3 Tbsp. of Greek Yogurt (Fat-Free)*
- *One tablespoon of Butter*

For the glaze:

- *Two Tbsp. Of Powdered Sweetener*
- *Half tablespoon of Water*

Directions: In a mixing bowl, add nutmeg, flour, baking powder, sugar alternative, cinnamon, and salt. Mix it well. With the help of a fork, slice the butter until crumbly.

Add the chopped apple and coat well, then add fat-free Greek yogurt.

Keep stirring until everything together, and a crumbly dough forms.

Put the dough on a clean surface and with your hands, knead it into a ball form.

Flatten the dough in an oval shape about a half-inch thick. It is okay, even if it's not the perfect size or shape.

Spray the basket of the air fryer with cooking spray generously. Put the dough in the air fryer for 12-14 minutes at 375ºF and cook until light golden brown.

For making the glaze mix, the ingredients, and with the help of a brush, pour over the apple fritter when it comes out from the air fryer. Slice and serve after cooling for 5 minutes.

Nutrition: Calories: 200.3, Protein: 9.8g, Carbs: 12.5g, Fat: 10.2g

Cheesecake Bites

Preparation Time: 40 minutes
Cooking Time: 2 minutes
Servings: 4

Ingredients:

- *½ cup almond flour*
- *½ cup and 2 tbsp. erythritol sweetener, divided*
- *4 oz. cream cheese, reduced-fat, softened*
- *½ tsp. vanilla extract, unsweetened*
- *2 tbsp. heavy cream, reduced-fat, divided*

Directions: Place the softened cream cheese in a bowl, add heavy cream, vanilla, and ½ cup sweetener, and whisk using an electric mixer until smooth.
Scoop the mixture on a baking sheet lined with a parchment sheet, then place it in the freezer for 30 minutes until firm.
Place flour in a small bowl and stir in the remaining sweetener.
Turn on the air fryer, insert the fryer basket, grease it with olive oil. Then close it with its lid, set the fryer at 350°F, and preheat for 5 minutes.
In the meantime, cut the cheesecake mix into bite-size pieces and coat it with almond flour mixture.
Open the fryer, add cheesecake bites, and cook for 2 minutes.
Serve straight away.

Nutrition: Calories: 197.8, Carbs: 5.6g, Fat: 17.9g, Protein: 3.3g, Fiber: 0g

Air Fryer Blueberry Muffins

Preparation Time: 10 minutes
Cooking Time: 12 minutes
Servings: 8

Ingredients:

- *Half cup of sugar alternative*
- *One and 1/3 cup of flour*
- *1/3 cup of oil*
- *Two teaspoons of baking powder*
- *1/4 teaspoon of salt*
- *One egg*
- *Half cup of milk*
- *2/3 cup of frozen and thawed blueberries, or fresh*

Directions: Let the air fryer preheat to 330 F.

In a large bowl, sift together sugar alternative, baking powder, salt, and flour. Mix well.

In another bowl, add milk, oil, and egg. Mix it well.

Combine the dry ingredients to the egg mixture, and mix. Add the blueberries and pour the mixture into muffin paper cups.

Cook muffins for 12-14 minutes and let them cool before serving.

Nutrition: Calories: 210.5, Protein: 9.2g, Carbs: 12.8g, Fat: 9.8g

Air Fryer Sugar-Free Lemon Cookies

Preparation Time: 5 minutes
Cooking Time: 5 minutes
Servings: 24 cookies

Ingredients:

- *Half teaspoon of salt*
- *Half cup of coconut flour*
- *Half cup of unsalted butter softened*
- *Half teaspoon of liquid vanilla stevia*
- *Half cup of swerve granular sweetener*
- *One tablespoon lemon juice*
- *Two egg yolks*

For icing:

- *Three tsp of lemon juice*
- *2/3 cup of Swerve confectioner's sweetener*

Directions: In a stand mixer bowl, add coconut flour, salt and Swerve. Mix until well combined.

Then add the butter (softened) to the dry ingredients, and mix well. Add all the remaining ingredients but do not add in the yolks yet. Adjust the seasoning of lemon flavor and sweetness to your liking.

Add the yolks and combine well.

Lay a big piece of plastic wrap on a flat surface, put the batter in the center, roll around the dough and make it into a log form, for almost 12 inches. Keep this log in the fridge for 2-3 hours or overnight, if possible.

Let the oven preheat to 325°F. Spray the air fryer basket, and take the log out from plastic wrap.

Cut in 1/4 inch cookies, place them in the air fryer basket, but do not overcrowd the basket.

Bake for 3-5 minutes. Let it cool in the basket for two minutes, then take out.

Once all cookies are baked, pour the icing over.

Nutrition: Calories: 65.4, Protein: 1.3g, Carbs: 1.9g, Fat: 5.6g

Coconut Pie

Preparation Time: 5 minutes
Cooking Time: 45 minutes
Servings: 6

Ingredients:

- *½ cup coconut flour*
- *½ cup erythritol sweetener*
- *1 cup shredded coconut, unsweetened, divided*
- *¼ cup butter, unsalted*
- *1 ½ tsp. vanilla extract, unsweetened*
- *eggs, pastured*
- *1 ½ cups milk, low-fat, unsweetened*
- *¼ cup shredded coconut, toasted*

Directions: Set the air fryer at 350°F, and preheat for 5 minutes.
Meanwhile, place all the ingredients in a bowl and whisk until blended and smooth batter comes together.
Take a 6-inches pie pan, grease with oil, then pour in the prepared batter and smooth the top.
Open the fryer, place the pie pan in it, and cook for 45 minutes until pie has set and inserted a toothpick into the pie slide out clean.
Let pie cool until garnish with toasted coconut Then cut into slices and serve.

Nutrition: Calories: 235.8, Carbs: 15.6g, Fat: 15.7g, Protein: 3.3g, Fiber: 2g

Chocolate Brownies

Preparation Time: 10 minutes
Cooking Time: 36 minutes
Servings: 4

Ingredients:

- *½ cup chocolate chips, sugar-free*
- *1 tsp. vanilla extract, unsweetened*
- *¼ cup erythritol sweetener*
- *½ cup butter, unsalted*
- *eggs, pastured*

Directions: Set the air fryer at 350°F, and preheat for 10 minutes.
Place butter and chocolate in a heatproof bowl and microwave for 1 minute, stirring every 30 seconds.
Crack eggs in another bowl, beat in vanilla and sweetener until smooth, and then slowly beat in melted chocolate mixture until well incorporated.

Take a springform pan that fits into the air fryer, grease it with oil, and then pour in batter in it.

Place the pan in the air fryer, close with its lid, and cook for 35 minutes until cake is done.

When the air fryer beeps, open its lid, take out the pan and let the brownies cool in it.

Then take out the brownies, cut them into even pieces, and serve.

Nutrition: Calories: 223.7, Carbs: 2.8g, Fat: 22.9g, Protein: 4.2g, Fiber: 1g

Spiced Apples

Preparation Time: 5 minutes
Cooking Time: 17 minutes
Servings: 4

Ingredients:

- *4 small apples, cored, sliced*
- *2 tbsp. erythritol sweetener*
- *2 tsp. apple pie spice*
- *2 tbsp. olive oil*

Directions: Set the air fryer at 350°F, and preheat for 5 minutes.

Place apple slice in a bowl, sprinkle with sweetener and spice, and drizzle with oil. Stir until evenly coated.

Add apple slices in the air fryer, close with its lid and cook for 12 minutes, shaking halfway through the frying. Serve straight away.

Nutrition: Calories: 89.2, Carbs: 21.2g, Fat: 1.8g, Protein: 0.8g, Fiber: 5.3g

Crustless Cheesecake

Preparation Time: 5 minutes
Cooking Time: 10 minutes
Servings: 2

Ingredients:

- *16 oz. cream cheese, reduced-fat, softened*
- *2 tbsp. sour cream, reduced-fat*
- *¾ cup erythritol sweetener*
- *1 tsp. vanilla extract, unsweetened*
- *2 eggs, pastured*
- *½ tsp. lemon juice*

Directions: Set the air fryer at 350°F, and preheat for 5 minutes.

Take two 4 inches of springform pans, grease them with oil, and set them aside.

Crack the eggs in a bowl and then whisk in erythritol, lemon juice, and vanilla until smooth.

Whisk in cream cheese and sour cream until blended and then divide the mixture evenly between prepared pans.

Place springform pans in the air fryer and cook for 10 minutes.

Take out the cakes, and refrigerate for 3 hours before serving.

Nutrition: Calories: 317.9, Carbs: 0.9g, Fat: 29.1g, Protein: 12.1g, Fiber: 0g

Chocolate Cake

Preparation Time: 5 minutes
Cooking Time: 15 minutes
Servings: 6

Ingredients:

- *¼ cup coconut flour*
- *1 tsp. baking powder*
- *⅓ cup Truvia sweetener*
- *¼ tsp. salt*
- *2 tbsp. cocoa powder, unsweetened*
- *1 tsp. vanilla extract, unsweetened*
- *2 tbsp. butter, unsalted, melted*
- *eggs, pastured*
- *½ cup heavy whipping cream, reduced-fat*

Directions: Set the air fryer at 350°F, and preheat for 5 minutes.

Take a 6 cups muffin pan, grease it with oil, and set aside.

Place melted butter in a bowl, whisk in sweetener until blended, and then beat in eggs, vanilla, and heavy whipping cream until combined.

Add remaining ingredients, beat again until incorporated and smooth batter comes together. Then pour the mixture into the prepared pan.

Place the pan in the air fryer and cook for 10 minutes.

Let the cake cool and serve.

Nutrition: Calories: 191.9, Carbs: 7.8g, Fat: 15.8g, Protein: 4.3g, Fiber: 2g

Chocolate Lava Cake

Preparation Time: 5 minutes
Cooking Time: 13 minutes
Servings: 2

Ingredients:

- *1 tbsp. flax meal*
- *½ tsp. baking powder*
- *1 tbsp. cocoa powder, unsweetened*
- *½ tbsp. erythritol sweetener*

- *⅛ tsp. Stevia sweetener*
- *⅛ tsp. vanilla extract, unsweetened*
- *1 tbsp. olive oil*
- *2 tbsp. water*
- *1 egg, pastured*

Directions: Set the air fryer at 350°F, and preheat for 5 minutes.
Meanwhile, take two cups of the ramekin, grease it with oil, and set it aside.
Place all the ingredients in a bowl, whisk until incorporated, and pour the batter into the ramekin.
Open the fryer, place ramekin in it, close with its lid, and cook for 8 minutes until inserting a skewer into the cake slides out clean.
Let the cake cool before cutting into slices, and serve.

Nutrition: Calories: 362.1, Carbs: 3.2g, Fat: 32.9g, Protein: 12.1g, Fiber: 0.6g